PRAISE FOR "B

"Donna Nielsen's book, B
heritage of marriage customs...with wonderful and careful scholarship, detailing the meaning of the marriage covenant to the Jews in those days. Those traditions give deep meaning to the Savior's teaching and to our hope that he will one day return." S.M., *Salt Lake City, Utah*

"The main thing I look for when I read is, "What does this teach me about the personality of the Savior?"...Certain passages stand out in my mind from *Beloved Bridegroom* where I felt a window open up and WOW there was a knowledge and witness of the Savior which become written in my heart. The (book's) insights into sexual union are absolutely priceless. How I want my children to learn this, the Lord's perspective, rather than the world's." P.M., *Lakeview, Oregon*

"Yours is the first LDS book that I have read in a long, long time that has had so much depth. You go into the *pshat*, *dresh*, and *remez* on this subject and yet present it with simplicity, clarity and understanding...The run of the mill writers appeal only to feelings and present ideals that they never get around to explaining how to accomplish. They are unlike the Jewish writer who will look into every single aspect of a subject and worry it to death and then look into each letter, each word, each phrase, where it is found, what comes before and what comes after...and then search out what all the past sages have said on the subject. Your book is full of (such) depth. You left me a lot to ponder. How Jewish of you." J.C., *Tucson, Arizona*

"Thank you for really explaining to me what the secret of women is: they are holy temples through which the love of God is manifest. Men have to be righteous priesthood holders so they don't defile the temple of a woman. These concepts (that you present) are so powerful and so full of wonderful symbolism that they must be taught especially to our young people."
M.G., *Salt Lake City, Utah*

BELOVED BRIDEGROOM

DONNA B. NIELSEN

Unless otherwise noted, Scripture quotations are from the Holy Bible, King James Version. Other quotations are taken from the Jewish New Testament Copyright © 1979, 1989, 1990, 1991, 1994, 1995 by David H. Stern. All rights reserved;The Living Bible, Verses marked TLB are taken from The Living Bible, copyright © 1971. Used by permission of Tyndale House Publishers, Inc., Wheaton, Illinois 60189. All rights reserved; New International Version - The Women's Devotional Bible © 1990 Scripture taken from the HOLY BIBLE, NEW INTERNATIONAL VERSIONS ®. Copyright © 1973, 1978, 1984 by International Bible Society. Used by permission of Zondervan Publishing House. All rights reserved; New Jerusalem Bible, Biblical text © 1985 by Darton, Longman & Todd Ltd and Doubleday, a division of Bantam Doubleday Dell Publishing Groups, Inc.; New Living Translation, Scripture quotations marked (NLT) are taken from the Holy Bible, New Living Tanslation, copyright © 1996. Used by permission of Tyndale House Publishers, Inc., Wheaton, Illinois 60189. All rights reserved; Revised Standard Version, Copyright 1952, by Division of Christian Education of the National Council of the Churches of Christ in the United States of America. New Testament Section, Copyright 1946, by Division of Christian Education of the National Council of the Churches of Christ in the United States of America; TANAKH - The New JPS Translation According to the Traditional Hebrew Texts, Copyright © 1985. Philadelphia • Jerusalem. Used by permission of The Jewish Publication Society. All rights reserved; Torah - Holy Scriptures according to the Masoretic Text © Copyright, 1981 by the Union of American Hebrew Congregations. New York. The English translation of The Torah, published and copyrighted © 1962, 1967 by the Jewish Publication Society; Holy Bible - King James Version with Joseph Smith Translation© Copyright 1979, 1981 by Corporation of the President of The Church of Jesus Christ of Latter-day Saints. Salt Lake City, Utah, U.S.A. All rights reserved; Book of Mormon© Copyright 1979, 1981 by Corporation of the President of The Church of Jesus Christ of Latter-day Saints. Salt Lake City, Utah, U.S.A. All rights reserved; Doctrine and Covenants © Copyright 1979, 1981 by Corporation of the President of The Church of Jesus Christ of Latter-day Saints. Salt Lake City, Utah, U.S.A. All rights reserved.

BELOVED BRIDEGROOM Copyright © 1999 by Onyx Press. Printed and bound in the United States of America. All rights reserved. No part of this book may be reproduced in any form or by any electronic or mechanical means including information storage and retrieval systems without permission in writing from the publisher, except by a reviewer, who may quote brief passages in a review.

ISBN # 1-57636-075-X

Cover Design: Tom Cryer
Cover Art: Todd Stilson
Interior Illustrations: Todd Stilson, Anthony Phan, Tom Cryer

Comments can be e-mailed to author: onyxpress@earthlink.net

PREFACE

Christ has many titles which describe the various aspects of His nature and power. He is called the Lamb, the Good Shepherd, the Bread of Life, the Light of the World, to name a few. The focus of this book relates to another scriptural title—the Bridegroom. *Beloved Bridegroom* has been written for those who want to better understand this metaphor in the scriptures, but have limited time for study and less access to helpful resources.

This is the book I was looking for when I wanted to learn more about this subject. I've attempted to compile information from many different sources into one user-friendly volume, while giving a general consensus from reputable scholars. I here express my heartfelt appreciation for the many biblical historians and linguistic experts whose extensive efforts made this compilation possible. I feel an immense debt of gratitude for their conscientious scholarship and painstaking research. A selected bibliography of those books I found especially useful appears at the end.

Studying this aspect of the Lord's ministry has given me great joy and has also increased my love and appreciation for the Savior. It is my hope that the information in this book will lead to a similar blessing the lives of those who read it.

ACKNOWLEDGEMENTS

From the bottom of my heart, I would like to thank Lisa Kovalenko Phan for being the most gifted literary midwife on the planet. Her contributions to this book include keen insight, talented typing, creative editing, organizational genius, unfailing support, cheerful cheerleading, musical entertainment, yummy lunch breaks, materials procurement, and an amazing can-do attitude. Some of my best memories have been made while we "feasted on the word" together. Lisa, this book exists, in so many ways, because of you. Thanks for sharing this adventure with me. You will eternally be a precious and cherished friend.

For giving me continuing encouragement and validation at a critical period in the composition of this book, I will forever be grateful to Mrs. Alta Barber. Thanks, Alta, for believing I could do this. You were just the jump start I needed.

For generously sharing their editing skills and giving me helpful feedback, I'd like to thank Pam and Cliff Mayes, Harry Russell, Karen Boren, Bob and Carol Norman, Scott and Laura Cook, Debbie Gordon, Linda Soderquist, and Dan and Carol Stephan. Carol generously took the time to check every scriptural reference.

To my parents, Donald and Elouise Burkhalter, I express deep gratitude. Their acceptance of the Restored Gospel brought great blessings to their posterity and their testimonies of Christ have been guiding lights in my life.

To my dear mother-in-law, Thelma Nielsen, who made numerous delicious dinners and occupied Michael in fun and interesting ways, I give great thanks. Your example of service is a continuing inspiration to me.

And finally thanks to my husband Sherm who has loved me, encouraged me, prayed for me, and never once complained.

FOREWORD
Dr. Robert J. Norman

When we read about Jesus and what he taught, we must remember that he was a Jew, teaching Jews, in a Jewish setting, using Jewish points of reference. As we increase our familiarity with the Jewish mind and culture, we more readily grasp the expansive nature of Christ's teachings. There is no substitute for coming to understand the times, customs, language, and setting of the Savior's ministry.

The wedding ceremony was a metaphor often used by Christ and the Old Testament authors. A study of Jewish marriage customs yields a wealth of spiritual understanding and deeper insight into the teachings of Jesus and the Biblical prophets.

One of the most emotional and powerful lessons relating to this topic in the Old Testament is found in the life of Hosea the prophet. The drama unfolds in the marriage and family of Hosea, his wife Gomer, and their three children. In this setting, Hosea is a type for Christ and Gomer is a symbol for Israel. Each of the children in the story are named to correspond with the relationship then developing between God and his covenant people Israel. As Gomer chooses to become a harlot and then leaves her husband and family, the reader begins to identify with the wrenching pain Hosea feels as he loses his cherished wife and lover to the ways of the wicked world–very much the way the Lord feels when his beloved covenant people abandon him and their sacred covenants.

What He requires of his people is expressed in Hosea 6:6

> *For I desired mercy, and not sacrifice; and the knowledge of God more than burnt offerings.*

Because it is translated from Hebrew into English, the true

meaning is lost to the reader. The Lord expresses that he wants *mercy* instead of sacrifice and *knowledge* instead of burnt offerings. Why would God desire mercy from *us*? I could never understand this verse until I took a Hebrew class. An explanation of the original Hebrew brought a flood of light to the question.

The word for "mercy" is "*hesed*" and refers to the deep spiritual and emotional bond that exists between two very close people such as husband and wife. Immediately, one perceives that God wants us to be as emotionally and spiritually close to him in thought and action as a devoted husband and wife would be. The word "knowledge" comes from two Hebrew words "*yada*" and "*daat*" both of which mean "to learn by close experience." Again, the Lord reinforces the idea that he desires to have a personal and intimate association with each individual. It is a humbling moment when we realize that such a powerful, loving, and kind God wants this type of a relationship. Such knowledge inspires one to "grow up" spiritually and to think more about the impact his life has on God.

This book is a rich resource for interpreting the cultural context of many well-known but little understood Hebrew customs. The reader can have many "ah hah" experiences as a relationship between ancient marriage rituals and latter-day temple worship becomes obvious. When reading by the Spirit, the "eyes of one's understanding" can be opened. The reflective reader cannot fail to gain a fresh sense of appreciation for the Savior and the beauty of his atonement. The scope of this book is nearly encyclopedic as it explores the significance of each step in the ancient marriage covenant.

It is my belief that husbands and wives who ponder these Biblical wedding and family customs in the context of their own marriages will find deeper meaning and more satisfaction in their relationships–both between themselves and with their children. The insights found in this book concerning the sanctity of life and the blessings of procreation can be a springboard for many thoughtful conversations.

Having taught religion for more than thirty years, I regret that I did not have this book when I was starting out. It would have matured and molded my scriptural understanding much earlier. I highly recommend this book as a source of spiritual understanding for every thoughtful gospel student.

Front Cover Illustration Note

This book cover was designed by Tom Cryer, author of *Visual Testament*. It is modeled after a Jewish wedding contract (*Ketuba*) and has several symbolic elements. Blue is the color anciently associated with priesthood. The arched window shape is called a Jerusalem window. The two doves are symbolic and denote a home of peace and fidelity. The red and green design features pomegranates cut in cross section to reveal multiple inner seeds. In Jewish thought, pomegranates have an association with the clothing of the High Priest (Exodus 28: 33-34), and also because of their many seeds, with the promises of Abraham, Isaac, and Jacob (Genesis 15:5). The crown is a standard decoration on marriage contracts, symbolizing that the married couple reign in their own home as a king and a queen. Of course, it is fitting also because Jesus Christ, our Savior, is the King of Kings. The red jewels in the crown represent the great drops of blood that were associated with the Atonement. Those who come unto him shall become "as stones of a crown, lifted up as an ensign upon his land (Zechariah 9:16).

Normally in the center (where the portrait of Christ is) the terms of the wedding contract are written. Accepting Jesus as the Christ and keeping all of his commandments are the terms we must accept to be saved in the Kingdom of Heaven.

DEDICATION

This book is dedicated to my five children—Amy, Robert, John, April, and Michael. My dear loved ones, it is my prayer that each of you will follow in His path with faith and joy, remembering always that:

> *The LORD your God is with you,*
>   *he is mighty to save.*
> *He will take great delight in you,*
>   *he will quiet you with his love,*
>   *he will rejoice over you with singing.*
>   Zephaniah 3:17 (NIV)

CONTENTS

Preface	i
Acknowledgements	ii
Foreword - Dr. Robert J. Norman	iii
Front Cover Illustration Note	v
Dedication	vi
Chapter One - Family Life in Israel	1
Roles of men and women, religious training of children, and family loyalty	
Chapter Two - The Marriage Proposal	11
Finding a mate, fire, desirable personal qualities, negotiating the bride price	
Chapter Three - The Bride's Acceptance	24
Ketubah, gift, ratify covenants, cup of wine, veil	
Chapter Four - Preparing a Place	33
Father's supervision, bride's preparations, double invitation, procession	
Chapter Five - The Ten Bridesmaids	46
Light, outer darkness, the father's house, closing the door	
Chapter Six - The Wedding Canopy	51
Wedding garments, crown of glory, seven bridal blessings	

Chapter Seven - Gardens and Fountains 61
  The sanctity of sexuality, scriptural euphemisms,
  spiritual views, wedding chamber

Chapter Eight - Food for Feasting 68
  Seven species, wedding song, party manners,
  etiquette

Chapter Nine - Song for the Bridegroom 95
  Prophetic principles, celebrating life stages,
  biblical prosperity, peace in the home

Chapter Ten - Spiritual Betrothal 107
  Christ paid the bride price, gift of the Sabbath,
  honoring his name

Chapter Eleven - Spiritual Preparation 121
  and Marriage
  The Comforter, Sabbath bride, cup of joy, knowing
  God, rending the veil

Chapter Twelve - The Imperative 145
  of Fruitfulness
  Bringing forth fruit, vessels, glory, holy places,
  brides in scripture

Appendix I 162
Appendix II 163
Glossary of Hebrew Terms 166
Index 169
Selected Bibliography 173
Praise for *Beloved Bridegroom* 185

CHAPTER ONE

Family Life in Israel

The world was newly created, fresh and beautiful. Indeed, God would declare it "very good." But it lacked a vital element.

After evaluating each creative period and finding them pleasing, the Lord then pronounced His very first *"not good."* It was *not* good that man should be alone. This did not mean that his state of aloneness was just less than desirable or mediocre, but that it was the worst possible situation. The language used is a very emphatic negative–meaning *not good in any way* (Leibowitz 10). For the ancient Hebrews, the word translated "alone" had overtones of separation and even of alienation. This would not do. The world's first marriage was the remedy. Eve was God's unique provision for Adam's aloneness–and he for hers.

Marriage was given of God from the beginning. Not only was it intended to make our individual lives happier and more secure, but like all other scriptural principles, it was designed to increase our love for and understanding of the Savior.

> *Behold, my soul delighteth in proving unto my people the truth of the coming of Christ; for, for this end hath the law of Moses been given; and* all *things which have been given of God from the beginning of the world, unto man,* are the typifying of him *(2 Nephi 11:4).*

Marriage is a beautiful type of the bond Christ longs to have with us.

> *For we are members of his body, of his flesh, and of his bones. For this cause shall a man leave his father and mother and be joined unto his wife, and they two shall be one flesh (Ephesians 5:30-31 NIV).*

When Jesus taught the people using examples of weddings and feasts, and of Himself as the Bridegroom, it was meaningful to them in a way that it is not to us because we lack understanding of their culture. The Bible was written by Jewish authors. They taught by using familiar events as examples that were easily understood by their listeners. Middle Eastern wedding customs had meanings for their ancient audience that are not always clear to us, and thus, many helpful insights are not readily apparent.

An knowledge of the Biblical marriage imagery can greatly enrich our understanding of how God relates to us through covenants. Biblical covenant marriage imagery encompasses principles as diverse as Sabbath observance, the Atonement, temple worship, and missionary work. It literally begins with Adam and ends with Zion.

There are many accounts that describe how marriages were conducted anciently. I chose to consider those elements of the ceremony which seemed to be the most universal. A wedding outline can be used as a model for explaining some of the ancient and modern customs and traditions. It can also serve as a pattern for establishing the type of Christ as the Bridegroom. (See Appendix I for the outline.) For instance, when we learn what the early Jewish wedding involved and apply that knowledge to the scriptures, the lights come on and then we can rejoice.

First of all, we need to understand that, according to Jewish tradition and law, marriage was not an option. It was the very first religious command given by God to man. A normal man was expected to be married.

The age for marriage was quite early in Israel. Most rabbis held that young people ought to be married by age eighteen, at the latest. They were often married younger than that. Technically, one month after his *Bar Mitzvah* (Son of the Law) at age thirteen, a boy was considered to be of marriageable age. For girls, the youngest acceptable age was twelve years and one month.

In the Jewish teachings, we read that: "A man who has no

wife is not a man. It is written that 'male and female created He them and blessed them and called *their* name Adam' (Genesis 5:2). Only with his wife does a man deserve the name of 'man'" (Jeb. 63a). Notice that the male and female shared the same name ...Adam.

Another quote concerning the importance of marriage states: "A man who has no wife is doomed to an existence without joy, without blessing, without true goodness, without atonement...without protection and without peace" (Yevamot 626). Truly, they thought a man would not receive the highest blessings that life offered without a woman by his side. Accordingly, the word for "salvation" in Hebrew—*jeshu-ah*—is a feminine term (JNTC-Stern 109). The Jews believed that marriage was an important element of salvation. Celibacy was not considered to be a virtue. There is not a word in Biblical Hebrew for "bachelor." Even the modern Hebrew word for bachelor, *ravak*, comes from a root word meaning "empty."

Members of the ruling body of the Jews, the Sanhedrin, were required to be married and to have children (Sanhedrin 36b), because they were then thought to have an increased capacity to show mercy. All Levites and members of the Priesthood were strongly encouraged to be married. The High Priest had to be married in order to carry out his functions in the temple, especially on Yom Kippur, the Day of Atonement, which was the most sacred day of the year.

At that time, the High Priest had to enter the Holy of Holies and invoke God's pardon for the people and effect purification for himself and *his house* (Leviticus 16:6). The definition of a house in the Jewish mind naturally included the Temple. But there is another interesting meaning. We are told in the Mishnah (Yoma 2a), that for a husband "his house, *his wife* —she is his house." So literally, from a Jewish frame of reference, a man without a wife was homeless.

The Jewish bride was consecrated to her groom and she became holy to him by virtue of that consecration. As a result, their relationship was expected to conform to high standards. These "duties of the heart" included mutual respect, devotion, chaste conduct, and kindness.

To the Jews in the time of Jesus, weddings conveyed much higher thoughts than just festivities and merriment. The relationship of the husband and wife was a type and was equated with the bond between Jehovah and His people. The bridal pair on their wedding day symbolized the union of God and Israel at Sinai. (This will be discussed in more detail in a later chapter.)

Preparation for this important event began at birth. When a little boy was born to a Jewish family, it was an occasion of great rejoicing and considered to be the highest blessing they ever hoped to receive. The baby was often affectionately called the "little bridegroom." This reflected one of three great hopes that parents had for their children, namely that their children would: study Torah (study the scriptures), be under the wedding canopy (marry in the covenant), and do good deeds (live righteous lives).

A daughter was not quite received with so much rejoicing. In some areas of the Middle East, a female birth was practically a cause for mourning. But of course, the little girls grew to win the hearts of both parents, and they found great delight in their daughters as well.

The ideal family life was considerate, respectful, and loving. Like the children in Israel today, they called their parents *Imma* and *Abba* (Mama and Daddy). In this environment, the little ones were carefully taught from an early age about their social and religious responsibilities. Especially emphasized were the importance of family loyalty, respect for elders, and obedience to parents. The Hebrew word for parent, *horeh*, derives from the root *yareh*, which means teaching, instruction, and direction (Wilson 216). The three most essential requirements for parents were: to love God, remember His commandments at all times, and then teach them to their children at every possible opportunity. This obligation was taken very seriously.

Until the age of three, the education of the family was mainly the responsibility of the mother. When a child turned three, the father became the primary source of information concerning the history of their people and the laws regarding correct behavior. Deuteronomy 32:7 reflects this and counsels children to "ask thy father and he will tell thee." The father was expected to know and live the law and to "make it known to the children and their children's children."

> The word *Torah* in Hebrew does not only mean "law", it also means "teaching". Moreover, the root for "Torah" can be traced to the Hebrew word meaning "to shoot an arrow," or "to hit the mark." Thus, the word "Torah" means literally, "teaching," whether it is the wise man instructing his son, or God instructing Israel. Hence, we can say that "Torah" is God's teaching, hitting the mark of man's needs, including his need to know who God is and what His righteousness looks like (Berkowitz 7).

To know and live the law required much diligence. Through a careful study of 5,845 verses in the first five books of the Bible (the Torah), the Jews found 613 commandments. These were the basis of the Law of Moses. When Christ was questioned about which of these 613 statutes was most important, he quoted Deuteronomy 6:4-5:

> *"Hear, O Israel: The LORD our God, is One Lord. And thou shalt love the Lord with all thine heart, and with all thy soul, and with all thy might."*

This scripture is called the *Shema* (pronounced as Shma) which means HEAR! or LISTEN! or PAY ATTENTION! This was the very first and most important religious principle that a child was taught. He memorized it and recited it several times daily. It gave him a true understanding of God compared to the polytheism so common in the surrounding cultures.

The *shema* was written on parchment, rolled up, and placed in a small cylinder called a *mezuza* which was fixed on the doorpost. A child was taught to kiss his fingers and touch the *mezuza* whenever entering or leaving the home. This action helped establish in the child's mind the importance of remembering the love of God in governing all his actions.

The principle of being a good listener is also emphasized in modern scripture. The first verse of Section 63 in the Doctrine and Covenants states:

> *"Hearken, O ye people, and open your hearts and give ear from afar; and listen, you that call yourselves the people of the Lord, and hear the word of the Lord and his will concerning you."*

This single verse contains five directives to hear the Lord's commands: "Hearken", "open your hearts" (spiritual ears), "give ear", "listen", and "hear." The two passages parallel each other beautifully.

> *Hear, O Israel...and these words...shall be in thy heart.*
> (Deut. 6:4-6)
> *Hearken, O ye people, and open your hearts...*(D&C 63:1)

In the Old and New Testament, "to listen" or "to hear" is the root for the idea of obedience. Both of the verses cited imply that truly hearing and heeding will naturally lead to improved behavior and greater love for the Lord. The importance of listening, hearing, and remembering can not be overstated, because the Hebrew culture was based on oral transmission of scripture. On the Sabbath, in the temple and in each synagogue, the same portion of the Torah was read aloud. The entire Torah was divided so that a complete reading was accomplished every three and a half years (Edershiem SJSL 277). By the time a person was middle-aged, the expectation was that they would have it committed to memory.

Besides scripture memorization, another educational tool used by parents is illustrated in Joshua 4:4-6. In this passage, the Lord instructs Joshua to have a representative from each of the twelve tribes take a stone from a dry riverbed (where a miracle had just taken place) and to pile them up together so that "when your children ask their fathers in time to come saying 'what mean ye by these stones?'...these stones shall be for a memorial unto the children of Israel forever."

This is a good example of how they used the natural curiosity of children to provide the best motivation for learning.

> First, the child was shown a symbol or a ritual to stimulate his interest.
> Next, the meaning was first explained by using a historical reference.
> Lastly, the child was taught the personal significance of the event for his life—to liken it unto himself.

It is interesting that the sentence, "What mean ye by these stones?" can also be translated from the Hebrew as, "What do these stones mean *to you?*" This last question offered the father an opportunity to bear a personal witness of the Lord's involvement in his own life and to teach his child to seek and expect similar experiences.

As a general rule, the boys received more formal education. They were instructed at the "house of the book," where they would sit in a semi-circle on the floor facing the teacher. The teacher was required to be a married man so that he could act as a proper role model. Most of the teaching was done by repetition and memorization. The scriptures were their only textbooks until the age of fifteen when instruction in Jewish law began. In addition to their schooling, each boy was required to learn a trade to support his future family.

Each girl grew up with the expectation that she would find fulfillment as a wife and a mother. At a young age, she became skilled in the homemaking arts. Her activities included learning how to spin and weave, cook meals and bake bread, help to tend family flocks, shop in the market place for fruit, and go to the well in the cool of the evening to supply water for the family.

8 / FAMILY LIFE IN ISRAEL

She also learned the rules and responsibilities of running a religious household.

The young Jewish girl gained an understanding of her importance in the family because of what she was taught about her future role. We find that role listed in Genesis 2:18,20 as "helpmeet." In Hebrew, the word is "*ezar*" which literally means "a helper." It is used twenty-one times throughout the scriptures:

- Twice, it refers to Eve as the first woman.
- Three times, it refers to vital human assistance in times of extreme need. For example, it describes the action of someone who gives water to a person dying of thirst, or places a tourniquet on the arm of a bleeding man, thereby saving his life. In one of its verbal forms, it sometimes refers to a person who offers testimony in law court, and thus provides grounds for the defendant's exoneration and acquittal (Terrien 10).
- In the other sixteen places, it refers to God, who acts as Israel's "mighty helper", so there is absolutely no idea that this is an inferior position. It is a comparison that is very similar to the Savior's job description.

The word help "meet," *ezar* "*negedo*," means that which is conspicuous, in front of, or in full sight of. It possesses a full range of ideas–royalty, vigor, courage, efficiency, and adventurousness. The verbal root suggests achievement, pioneering, and risk taking–all appropriate descriptions relating to Eve's behavior (Terrien 11-adapted).

The girls were also reminded that "the wisdom of women builds the home" (Proverbs 14:1). In connection with the idea that women "build" a home, it is noteworthy that the Biblical Hebrew verb BNH (Strong 1129) "to build" had three main applications. In Genesis 2:22, it is the verb used when God created or built a woman. First, this had overtones of beauty, stability, and durability. She was literally "built to last." Second, it is an architectural term that is only used in relation to a very specific kind of building and its associated furnishings. That building is the temple. And third, it means to bear children. These are wonderful associations. You might say that children literally go through a *temple* when they are born. And that the birth of each child born in the covenant is *building* God's kingdom on the earth.

As a people, the Jews have survived intact for centuries because of their attitudes toward their families and their appreciation for the purity and stability of the home. It was believed that through prayer and praise, each home could reflect God's glory. The rabbis taught that the home, like the temple, was to be set apart for special purposes. These included the worship of God ("a house of prayer"), the learning of Torah ("a house of study"), and the serving of community needs ("a house of assembly"). In addition, just as the golden table of shewbread in the temple contained loaves of bread set in two rows (Exodus 25:23-30, and Leviticus 24:5-9), so also on Sabbath eve in the home, the mother set two loaves of bread on the table to symbolize God's sustaining presence (Wilson 215).

A mother's influence and contribution were invaluable for the happiness of the home. They believed that a faithful mother had a unique sensitivity to human nature and that she instinctively knew what was best for her young children. The scriptures seem to validate this understanding.

When it came time for Abraham and Sarah to make plans for the future of their son Isaac, the Lord advised Abraham in Genesis 21:12 that Sarah's counsel was correct and "in all that Sarah hath said unto thee, hearken unto her voice...." The translation from the Hebrew is even more direct: "Whatever Sarah tells you to do, do as she says." Great trust was placed in feminine discernment and in righteous motherhood.

When parents did their job well, the children matured and learned the importance of compliance with the religious traditions of obedience and family loyalty that governed life. A person's maturity was measured by how well he conformed to those traditions. The idea of independent nonconformity or "I did it *my way*" was repugnant. The only acceptable way was God's way.

When young people had completely absorbed this lesson, they were prepared to find a mate and take their place as adults in the community.

CHAPTER TWO

The Marriage Proposal

Our modern customs of dating and "falling in love" are in sharp contrast to the traditions of the ancient Israelites. We take it for granted that a young man can freely find a girl of his choice, and that a girl can freely date and accept a boy who is attractive to her. This process is encouraged by parents who often arrange and support opportunities to meet potential partners. Acquaintances are made through school and church activities, community functions, and sometimes through mutual employment and commercial activities. During the dating period, it is not uncommon for modern young people to have multiple "serious relationships" before they settle on a definite partner.

This kind of social freedom and independent mingling would have been bewildering and unappealing to the youth of Bible times who were raised with entirely different expectations and without the idea of a "social life" as we understand it. Most of the Israelite communities were quite small (this definitely limited the options), and the boys and girls were naturally kept segregated by their daily activities. There were only infrequent opportunities to view members of the opposite sex. A girl might see and be seen by the friends of her brothers and cousins at home or while tending sheep or fetching water from the village well. But she certainly would never have had any public conversations with members of the opposite sex. Such conduct would have caused gossip and damaged her personal and family reputation. There were never any public displays of affection such as hand holding and hugging–even between betrothed couples–and kissing was definitely an activity reserved exclusively for marriage.

Social activities involving the entire community provided some diversions for the youth of that day. Possibly the most enjoyable of all was the fall harvest festival. Everyone, young and old, participated in prolonged feasting, singing, dancing, and great rejoicing because the food supplies for the coming season had been replenished. It is difficult for us to truly appreciate the significance this event had for those people. We are accustomed to abundance and our worries regarding grain are very different. Today's farmer worries about not knowing where to store all the new wheat because he still has grain left from the previous year.

According to Middle Eastern scholar, George Lamsa, grain was often scarce in the Middle East, and seed for the coming season was carefully preserved by each individual farmer, because there was no other source from which to purchase them. Generally, the wheat supply was exhausted by the time spring came, and those spring months were the very most difficult for the Israelite families. Bread was carefully rationed at that time, and the children were sometimes hungry. There is a saying that describes the sorrow that fathers felt as they used the remaining grain for seed while their children were crying for bread. In Psalms 126:5, it says: "They that sow in tears shall reap in joy." The farmers would literally weep—tears streaming down their cheeks—as they scattered the precious seeds, but this act of faith was rewarded during the fall months (O.T. Light 538). "Rejoicing at harvest time" was a metaphor for the greatest rejoicing in life that could possibly be experienced. Many marriages were scheduled during this happy time. It was also during this period that the young girls would don white dresses to dance and sing, and sometimes a young man had a limited chance to surreptitiously observe eligible young women and possibly make a suggestion to his parents regarding a potential bride.

But the Hebrew young people had no expectations that the "right one" would be found through a process of dating many different people. Today we would find their perception of marriage more related to what we would consider a legal agreement between families rather than the concept of two young people who are "in love." It was not that love was thought to be unimportant, it was just that to them, love was an emotion to be cultivated *after* marriage rather than before. Much more emphasis was placed on the principle that marriage meant honoring a sacred commitment to a pledge. A person's word of honor to be loyal and to make the marriage work was considered more significant than passionate attraction. Although this seems unromantic by our standards, this total commitment formed a solid foundation for the couple's future relationship.

A contemporary minister and religious psychologist, Walter Trobisch, effectively summed up the differences between ancient and modern marriages. In stressing the need for love to come after marriage and not simply before, he quoted a Middle Eastern man who once said to a European, "We put cold soup on the fire and it becomes slowly warm. You put hot soup into a cold plate and it becomes slowly cold" (Wilson 202). It is interesting to see that this progressive concept is reflected even in the language. The Semitic root word for "love" is *haw* or *hav*. It means "to warm", "to kindle", "to set on fire." To the Hebrews, a "burning in the bosom" could be a manifestation of *love*. It is interesting that at Mt. Sinai (which the Jews think of as the place where God chose Israel as a covenant marriage partner), the mountain appeared to be on fire. This dramatic event naturally terrified the Israelites. But it is a sweet thought that perhaps the fire represents a level of love that we mortals cannot even comprehend. The truths that "God is love" (1 John 4:8) and that "He dwells in everlasting burnings" (Isaiah 33:14-15) are semantically related.

Just as the blazing fire at Mt. Sinai technically began with an experience at a small burning bush, the Hebrew view of marriage followed a pattern with kindness, amicability, and warmth at the beginning which naturally led, over time, to deeper emotional intimacy and eventually to greatly enhanced physical love and desire. The expectation was that a newly married young couple might start out with "sparking," but that they could eventually progress to marital "flame throwing!"

With this hope and anticipation for their future, most young people were generally content and grateful for parents who would arrange suitable matches for them. Jewish parents took this responsibility very seriously and considered it a sacred duty. [Matchmakers such as Yenta portrayed in *Fiddler on the Roof* were mostly used from the 11th to the 19th century. They became necessary because of the social disruption caused by persecution and dispersion.] However, at the time of Christ, this was definitely a parental assignment. Mothers (and aunts) of the groom would often lay the ground work and negotiate behind the scenes with the bride's mother, and, if no objections were raised, it became the father's obligation to take the formal public action that would finalize the matter.

Many factors were taken into consideration during this process. The children in a family could often hear these matters being discussed, so they knew that the decisions concerning their future were being made after much deliberation and with a definite desire for their welfare and happiness.

The daughter in a family had no personal initiative or choice in the matter of a husband. She was expected to trust in the good judgment of her parents and obey their wishes. But the law stated that she could not be forced to marry anyone who was distasteful to her. The most frequent cause for rejection was based on the type of employment a suitor had. For example, a tanner was considered extremely objectionable because of the smelly nature of his work. Generally, however, marriage and children were so important that she felt grateful for her opportunity to become a wife and have a family. There are interesting stories in the Bible relating just how far some women have been willing to go to have the experience of motherhood. (Genesis 19:30-38, and all of Genesis 38)

The personal qualities that are considered beautiful vary from culture to culture, but there were some attributes that every young Jewish man longed for his wife to possess. Usually, a prospective bride would be looked over by the groom's mother, sisters, or aunts, and her features were then duly reported to the family. Young girls were counseled to show a meek and quiet demeanor when they wanted to make a good impression. A good wife was thought to be intelligent, modest, wise ("A wife who honors her husband is accounted wise"), obedient, and charming ("A wife's charm is the delight of her husband/and her knowledge puts flesh on his bones"). And for a maximum positive effect, they were urged to sit up straight with their chins pressed down against their chests to give the effect of a double chin. Women of generous dimensions were highly praised and appreciated. Ample hips and large bosoms were especially valued traits. In some areas, even today, men long to brag that their wives have to go through the door sideways. This is the supreme masculine boast guaranteed to engender envy among his peers.

Besides the desired physical appearance, it was also most important that a bride under consideration share common origins with her future husband and have a strong belief in the God of Israel. To marry outside of the covenant was to invite marital and spiritual disaster.

To find a suitable bride was an especially difficult matter for the nomadic desert dweller. Abraham, for example, having renounced city life, was obliged to send a trusted servant on a very long journey to find an appropriate wife for his son, Isaac. The name of this servant is thought by many modern scholars to be Eliezar (meaning: God is my helper). Significantly, the ancient Jews saw their role regarding the marriage of their children as being associated with God's prior assignment of a mate for every individual born into this world. Each righteous parent hoped that God would inspire them and approve of their choice. They recognized that blending two lives was a serious and challenging matter.

A Roman woman once asked a rabbi what God had been doing since He finished the creation of the earth. The rabbi replied that God had been occupied since then with making matches, and it was a task as difficult as dividing the Red Sea.

16 / A MARRIAGE PROPOSAL

Surely, Eliezar also saw his assignment as daunting. We are told in Genesis that after being charged with the responsibility of selecting a suitable spouse for Isaac, that Eliezar offered the first recorded prayer requesting divine guidance (Genesis 24:12) and then decided upon a character test for the potential bride.

Upon his arrival in Haran, Eliezar went to the most likely place to view the girls of the village. Twice a day, the women went to the well to obtain the water necessary for cooking, washing, and watering the family animals. The young girls of that time who were not yet betrothed could be recognized by their long unbound hair and their lack of a veil. Their financial status was often evidenced by the sort of container in which they carried water. The poorer women used pottery and the more well-to-do had brass vessels.

The test which the servant used is a good indicator of the traits which were the most highly valued in that society. His simple plan was to request a "sip" of water from a maiden. If the maiden was the predetermined bride-to-be, the sign was that she would be willing, and in addition, would also offer to water his camels.

When the beautiful Rebekah came up from the well, Eliezar ran to meet her and made his request for a drink. We don't know what kind of jar she carried, but her hospitable and considerate response showed that her inner beauty of character matched her lovely outward appearance. According to the oral tradition, her diligent efforts literally caused speechless amazement and wonder in Abraham's servant. The task of watering ten camels *until they had their fill* was difficult enough, but we are told in Genesis 24:16,20 that she had to go down into the well (often several dozen steps), draw the water, come up, empty the pitcher into the trough, and return again many times. Camels after a long journey are quite naturally depleted, and each camel can drink from ten to thirty gallons of water. This task on Rebekah's part–self-appointed–to quench the thirst of a stranger *and* his camels showed exemplary kindness, generosity, and hospitality and earned her a place in the hearts of the Jewish people forever.

No wonder that she was such a comfort and blessing from the very beginning to her husband Isaac.

Later, when Isaac himself was a father, he likewise stressed the importance of not intermarrying into the local Canaanite culture. In Genesis 28:1-2, Isaac charges his son Jacob to travel to Padan-Aram to marry from among his kindred. In those days, cousins were considered to be ideal matches. Because there was already a common family loyalty and bond that assured compatibility on social and economic levels, it was felt that the new marriage would have increased stability.

Only a disobedient and rebellious son would marry a woman of his own choice without the prior consent of his father. Whenever this happened, the results were never happy. When Esau chose and married two Hittite women without consulting his parents, it caused Isaac and Rebekah great bitterness and grief of mind (Genesis 26:34-35). Such an action generally caused the son to lose his position of respect and authority in the family and often resulted in the forfeiture of the birthright and his role as a spiritual leader and patriarchal head. If he was not responsible enough to seek a wife who would raise the children correctly (according to the beliefs of his people), then he lost the esteem of his extended family. Sad experience had shown that the non-Israelite spouse often turned the heart of the Israelite partner away from God to foreign deities. This was a dire situation affecting the well-being of unborn generations and was also considered a calamity for the community who looked upon every family as part of a larger corporate body. This idea is reflected in the later theology of Paul in the New Testament (I Corinthians 12:26) where he compares each member of the church to a part of a body. Each part was necessary for the well-being of the whole, and any weakness affected the entire body. Strength and unity in individual marriages strengthened the entire community.

Once the search for a suitable bride was resolved, negotiations to finalize the matter could commence. The wedding under Jewish law was very simple and had three parts that were very specifically outlined. The collective term for all that broadly comprises a Jewish marriage is *Kiddushin*, which literally means "sanctities." This concept includes ideas of being *devoted irrevocably*, being *sanctified and set apart*, and being *consecrated*. Marvin Wilson, in his book *Our Father Abraham* made this insightful comment:

> ...the joining of a man and a woman is a reenactment or replica of God's eternal covenant relation to his chosen. To understand Biblical marriage is to understand the Biblical concept of covenant. Marriage is a permanent covenant. In Hebrew 'to make a covenant' is literally 'to cut a covenant' (*karat berit*). [A ribbon-cutting ceremony reflects this understanding.] Biblical covenants were sometimes symbolized by cutting animals in two.
>
> The shedding of blood dramatically ratified and sealed the covenant (Genesis 15:9-18; Jeremiah 34:18-20). If one attempted to break the covenant, the blood served as a powerful visual lesson that one's own blood would be shed. In brief, it was a solemn oath to be kept on pain of death. It was thus inviolable and irrevocable (Wilson 205).

As we can see, the undertaking of a covenant commitment had serious implications. There were three parts that were vital to a completed marriage contract in Biblical times. These were *money*, *writ*, and *intercourse*. All three of these conditions had to be met for a marriage to be recognized as legal. These will be discussed in greater detail, but essentially, they referred to:

Money = *bride price*—a bride was acquired through money or services rendered.

Writ = *ketuba*—a contract wherein the groom consecrated himself to his future wife.

Intercourse = *"knowing" a wife*—This part filled the requirement that blood be shed as a fulfillment of the covenant.

When a young man was ready to take on this responsibility, he went to the home of his prospective bride, usually accompanied by his father or another close male family member. This male family member sometimes had the designation "friend of the bridegroom." (In Judea, there were two "friends": one assigned to the bride and one to the groom during the betrothal period.) With this title came several responsibilities. Not only would he accompany the groom to make his marriage "proposal," but his ongoing duties included delivering invitations to the wedding, acting as liaison between the bride-to-be and the groom during the betrothal period, watching over the needs of the bride in the groom's absence, becoming guarantor of the bride's virgin chastity until the consummation took place, being the governor at the marriage feast, and finally, his last obligation was announcing to the assembled guests that the full marriage was successfully "completed."

This "friend of the bridegroom" would give moral support to the groom at the momentous event of proposing marriage. They would also take two other witnesses with them as part of their delegation. An appointment was usually made for Wednesday night and virtually always in the middle of the month when there was a full moon because they thought that meant good luck. Wednesday was the fourth day of the week, and according to the book of Genesis, the day on which the sun, moon, and stars had been created.

When the delegation arrived at the bride's home, they were offered food and drink as a gesture of hospitality, but they refused to partake until their request had been granted and the bride gave her consent.

There is a scripture in Genesis 24:33 that faithfully reflects this protocol. When Eliezar went to the home of Laban to begin negotiations for Rebekah, it says:

> *And there was meat [food] set before him to eat: but he said, I will not eat, until I have told mine errand. And he said, Speak on.*

20 / THE MARRIAGE PROPOSAL

Middle Easterners have strong associations between covenants and the idea of a covenant meal to seal an agreement. Eating a covenant meal together in Biblical times was a way to ratify pacts or treaties. By consuming meals together, they symbolically became members of the same family. This was especially true regarding bread. Through partaking from the same loaf at the same table, even strangers became *companions*, a word whose literal meaning is "one with whom bread is broken." Some linguists believe that the Hebrew word for "covenant" (*berith*) possibly had its origin in the Hebrew word meaning "to eat with salt" (Juengst 17).

A frequent saying repeated by people from the Middle East is, "There is bread and salt between us," meaning that we are one by solemn agreement. To break a "bread and salt covenant" violates something that is considered sacred. It is a lasting stigma, forever branding one as untrustworthy.

It was not necessary to eat a full meal for a connection to occur. It could also be done by simply eating salt together. Eating salt with another was a way to indicate a bond of loyalty. God's promise to Aaron in Numbers 18:19 was described as a "covenant of salt," meaning an unbreakable or permanent covenant.

As a side note, there is another interesting illustration of salt in relationship to the covenant parents make with their child at birth. A very old custom is still practiced in some areas of the Middle East today. According to this custom, mothers first bathe their newborn infants, then gently rub a very small amount of salt that has been finely pulverized in a stone mortar for this great occasion. Middle Eastern parents believe that putting salt on the baby's body will make his or her flesh firm. This little ceremony also represents a symbolic testimony that the parents will raise the child to be truthful and faithful (Errico 80). In certain areas of the Middle East to make a remark that a person may not have been "salted" at his birth is to stir up a lot of trouble. Since symbolically salt represents faithfulness, such a comment reflects unfavorably on the person and on his family (See Ezekiel 16:3-4).

Even when Jesus spoke the words, *"have salt in yourselves,"* he may have been referring to the covenant of salt, reminding his disciples of the importance of their loyalty and devotion to one another. This is particularly significant in light of the last part of the sentence which says, *"and be at peace one with another"* (Mark 9:50). The admonition in Colossians 4:6 (*"Let your speech always be...seasoned with salt"*) may also refer to the symbolic power of salt to create unity and harmony because of the covenant (Juengst 52).

With so much importance attached to the idea of "breaking bread" or sharing a meal, no wonder that a food could not be eaten together until a binding contract between the bride and groom had been settled. George Lamsa has recorded that, for the negotiation process to begin today, the spokesperson for the delegation announces: "We have come to seek the hand of your daughter." If the father is pleased and agreeable he can say, "My daughter is a pair of shoes before your feet." [Note: This comment does *not* have the negative connotations for them that it has for us! More on "feet" and "covering" is mentioned in Chapter 7.]

The word for bride price and dowry (*mohar*) is found three times in the Old Testament: Genesis 34:12, Exodus 22:17, and I Samuel 18:25. In essence, the bride price is a payment rendered by the bridegroom or his family to the father and/or family of the bride. This is in accordance with the original (not present-day) meaning of the word, "wed." Earlier, it meant a pledge of money given by a man to seal his offer to marry. This was not like buying a slave but was perceived as compensating the father for the great loss of his daughter and her contribution to the household. It recognized the care and diligence required to raise her to be a suitable wife. In addition, it also sealed a bond of alliance between the two families and signified the transfer of authority from father to husband (Collins 113).

According to Raphael Patai, the payment of a bride price was not regarded as degrading by either family. On the contrary, the value and esteem of a woman were directly connected to the size of the bride price paid for her. It was expected that the more noble the family and the more beautiful the girl, the higher the bride price asked for her. Her strength, age, ability, and character determined the final amount. The price paid also influenced the level of esteem that the groom's family had for the bride. The lower the price, the less she was valued by her husband and his kin. If a man obtained a wife for a small price, he had little respect for her. But if much was paid for her, he felt he had something valuable, a person who had to be cherished and well treated (S & F 57).

The bride price was generally negotiated in the presence of the bride and her mother, while sitting around a table. This was frequently the first time the boy and girl had seen each other. Of course, the mother and daughter did not speak, but they were keenly interested in the proceedings.

At the beginning, the amount asked for by the bride's side and the one offered by the bridegroom's side were usually so far apart that it would appear that they could never come to a mutual agreement. It took patient negotiation—conducted with much skill, beseeching, and impressive promises—to successively narrow the gap and finally come to terms. The final price was frequently paid in livestock—especially in camels. A real beauty might qualify for four camels. Money and jewels were always acceptable, and service to the father could be substituted when funds were limited. In really desperate situations, the young man could appeal to the community for assistance. Helping a young person in this situation was thought to be an especially good deed.

Part of this bride price later became the woman's dowry, so that in the event of her husband's death, or if he divorced her, she was left with some financial security. A portion of the money was used by the father to purchase household utensils for his daughter. Sometimes an alabaster box or vial filled with fragrant ointment was given as a dowry item. (When the husband died, it was the custom to break the container, anoint the body with its contents, and then to leave the fragments of the jar in the tomb [Barclay 198].) The dowry also was used to purchase clothing for special occasions and jewelry, such as earrings, nose rings, bracelets, and gold coins. These would be worn constantly by the girl for the remainder of her life—her own personal possession—by law never to be taken as payment for any debt incurred by her husband. They were carefully guarded, both for their value and their symbolic meaning. This dowry had the root idea of "en-dower-ment" or endowment. To receive an endowment before her marriage from her father made the young girl feel protected and loved. It was a shield and safeguard against future uncertainty.

CHAPTER THREE

The Bride's Acceptance

The settlement of the bride price signified that the first stage of marriage had commenced. You'll recall that anciently, the marriage, *kiddushin*, consisted of two parts which were separated by a year or more. The first stage was betrothal or *erusin* which is related to the Hebrew root word *asar*, meaning "to bind" (Strong 781). Betrothal in the Jewish mind was a serious covenant, with a much greater idea of commitment than an engagement has today. Covenant relationships were final, sealed in blood, and legally binding. Betrothal was so legally binding that one could not break the contract without a divorce (*get* in Hebrew). During betrothal, a couple was considered legally married, even though the marriage was not yet consummated. This situation is reflected in Luke 2:5 where it states that Mary was the "espoused (betrothed) wife" of Joseph.

Joseph was described as a "just man," which was a current expression at the time for a strict observer of the Law (Geikie 111). The penalty for unfaithfulness during betrothal–stoning–was the same as for adultery after marriage. According to the *Mishnah* (Jewish law), adultery during the betrothal period is a more serious sin than adultery after marriage. This shows us how compassionate Joseph was, for when he first discovered that Mary was "with child," he planned to put her away (give her a *get*, a divorce) privately and quietly rather than making an example of her. He could have had her stoned, according to the penalty set forth in law, thereby putting her to public shame (Matthew 1:19).

Part of the reason the penalty was so severe was that in Bible times, after the bride price (*mohar*) was paid, a man was considered to own the woman. He had purchased her and she belonged to him. In ancient Israel, brides were considered a personal possession. The word for wife, *be'ulah*, literally means "owned one." Husband, or *ba'al* (also *adon*) means "owner" or "lord and master" (Vine 140). The tenth commandment reflects this understanding:

> *Thou shalt not covet thy neighbor's house, thou shalt not covet thy neighbor's wife, nor his man servant, nor his maid servant, nor his ox, nor his ass, nor anything that is thy neighbors* (Exodus 20:17).

In this listing, a wife is included as part of a man's possessions.

A modern mindset might find this concept of a woman being "owned" offensive, but it was actually a great improvement for the times, which increased the rights and protections a woman had. The pagan tradition was that when a man wanted to marry a woman, he took her to his house, and by the act of intercourse, she became his wife. There was no formal ceremony, no witnesses to a contract, and no family support. There was no permanent protection for the woman, her children, or the marriage. Under this custom, a man could divorce her by merely saying, "I now hate you," three times in the presence of witnesses. ["Hate" was a legal and technical term that meant "to repudiate" (Blenkinsopp 65; Collins 119, 154)]. The unfortunate wife had no legal recourse. In one move, she lost her husband, home, and her children.

The Jews were blessed because God gave them specific instructions for marriage in order to sanctify it as the most important unit of society. Under God's law, marriage had permanency and gave protection to both parties. In addition, it helped to strengthen the entire community. Although a woman was a "possession" of the husband, she was still considered to have an extremely significant place in his heart. The word used to describe this relationship is *segulah* (Strong 5459) which means "peculiar treasure" or "treasured possession" (see Exodus 19:5 for an example of this usage). *Segulah* was the term that kings used to identify certain objects in their possession that were carefully

26 / THE BRIDE'S ACCEPTANCE

guarded because of their great worth. *Segulah* also had overtones of being "hidden." Although kings valued all of their possessions, their special (peculiar) treasures were dearest to their hearts. Truly, the worth of a bride was great in the eyes of her husband. An official written agreement stressed this importance.

The terms of the marriage contract were spelled out in a formal document called a *ketubah*. The word means "that which is written," and it stated the bride price, spelled out the promises and obligations of the groom and listed the rights of the bride. It signified a permanent covenant and an exclusive commitment, and it also acted as a safeguard against hasty divorce (Cohen 168). The *ketubah* is a marriage contract that all bridegrooms are required to give their brides today at a Jewish wedding. Anciently, this was done at the time of negotiating the bride price. It is still considered so very important and binding that, if a couple ever loses their *ketubah*, they are forbidden to live together until a new one has been written.

The earliest known wedding contract was discovered in Egypt in 1905 and was dated back to about 440 B.C., not long after the Babylonian exile (Flaugher 34). The marriage contract (covenant) is not known by the name of *ketubah* in the Bible, but Biblical scholar Roland de Vaux, in his book *Ancient Israel*, maintains that there are at least three examples in the Old Testament which allude to this marriage contract:

> *Malachi 2:14 ...the wife of thy covenant*
> *Proverbs 2:17 ...The covenant of God...*
> *Ezekiel 16:8 ...Covenant of God...Sinai*

Anciently, the wording of this document varied slightly from area to area, but essentially the *ketubah* stated the groom's promises to the bride in language similar to this:

1. I will provide you with food, clothing, and necessities.
2. I will redeem you if you are ever taken captive.
3. I will live with you as a husband according to the universal custom.

A man's status in the community was largely determined by how well he fulfilled the first condition. Having a plump, well-dressed wife reflected favorably on the husband, indicating that he was successful and prosperous.

The second promise reflected the times when a woman could possibly be taken as a captive and sold for a slave. The word "redeem" means "to set free by paying a price." Any expense incurred by the woman's redemption could not be deducted from her dowry (Collins 111). The *ketubah* currently in use and given at modern Jewish weddings generally omits this phrase as irrelevant for today's circumstances.

Lastly, the phrase "live with you" is a Jewish euphemism for sexual relations. The religious leaders spelled out this contractual relation because they believed that most women would be too shy or modest to initiate this kind of behavior. They felt she needed protection from her husband in case he was not as interested in a sexual relationship as she would hope. It also insured fairness in times when polygamy was practiced and guaranteed that her sexual rights would not be ignored if she was older or less attractive than a more favored wife. This was an extremely important provision, especially during the child-bearing period, because children were a significant source of status in the community who helped to support her in her older years.

Jewish legal rules even legislated the minimal frequency of sexual relations based on a man's profession and the amount of time he could spend at home. The law regarding this matter stated: "Every day for those who have no occupation (independently wealthy), twice a week for laborers, once a week for ass-drivers; once every thirty days for camel-drivers; and once every six months for sailors" (Mishnah Ketubot 5:6; Ketubot 62b). A later work, the *Shulchan Aruch* additionally states that, "As for scholars, it is obligatory for them to have intercourse once a week, and it is customary for this to be on Friday nights."

A modern authority, Rabbi Louis Jacobs, has noted: "A husband cannot change his occupation without his wife's consent if this will affect her conjugal rights—from ass-driver to camel-driver, for instance—since it can be assumed that a wife will prefer to have her needs satisfied even if, as a result, her husband's earnings will be less" (cited by Telushkin 616). For many married couples, part of the Sabbath joy is to have relations on Friday night (Herzog 312).

Throughout Jewish history, artistic illuminated *ketubot* (plural of *ketubah*) have been created for prominent display in the couple's home. Anciently, the *ketubah* became the carefully guarded possession of the wife. It was read as a kind of "love letter" during the waiting period between betrothal and nuptials. A bride cherished her *ketubah* for both its meaning as a covenant and for its beauty. It was proof of her beloved's devotion and her inalienable rights.

The next stage in the marriage arrangement after the presentation of the *ketubah* was that the bridegroom would offer a token or pledge to the young woman. Historically, in the Jewish system, a "gift of value" was necessary to fulfill the requirement for a betrothal. In the ancient Middle East, the groom's gift was considered to be an actual extension of himself and indirectly established his authority over the bride (Sacks 75-76). It also symbolized his willingness to sacrifice and served as a reminder of his love.

A gold ring was frequently used as this token or gift because it represented eternity. Anciently, the ring used was often a link from a gold chain. The chain represented past and future family associations and was seen as symbolically linking the girl to her new family. Gold or silver coins were also considered suitable gifts. The value of whatever gift was given depended on the status of the bridegroom, but it had to be his own possession. It could not be something that he borrowed for the occasion or was paying off with payments. It had to be something he owned, free and clear.

It is thought that this "gift of value" is referred to by Christ when he told the parable of a woman who lost a coin. That parable (recounted in Luke 15:8) says, "Either what woman having ten pieces of silver, if she lose one piece, doth not light a candle, and sweep the house, and seek diligently until she find it?" The coin, although it had financial value, represented something far more significant than grocery money. Its loss would be the modern equivalent of losing a wedding ring. In Bethlehem, ten silver coins were a traditional wedding gift from the groom. These coins were worn on a chain which was attached to her veil as an important part of her headdress. A wife prized this gift and guarded it carefully because if she were careless, this might be interpreted by her husband as a lack of affection and respect for him. Sometimes, a husband would become very jealous and think that his wife had used the money to purchase a lover. (Unfortunately, there was historical precedent for this!) This mistaken belief might lead to divorce. So these coins were held sacred by the Jews, and the wife would use the money from this gift only in the event of divorce or widowhood. We can, then, understand the woman's concern and anxiety when she lost it and why she was so happy that she called her neighbors (her women friends) to rejoice with her when she found it.

The potential bridegroom, after offering this gift or token, recited a ritual statement to consecrate himself to his bride. One of these ritual statements can be found in Hosea 2:19-20.

And I will betroth thee unto me forever; yea, I will betroth thee unto me in righteousness, and in judgment, and in lovingkindness, and in mercies. I will even betroth thee unto me in faithfulness: and thou shalt know the Lord.

The word "consecrate," wherein the groom consecrated himself to the bride, is used to mean, "to devote irrevocably." The groom has no options here—no escape clauses—there is no question ever that he would rescind his invitation to the woman to marry her. He can not break this engagement if the woman remains faithful, for he is bound if she fulfills her part of the covenant.

The Jews had several ways to ratify covenants between two parties. One Old Testament way was to "walk the blood path." Sacrificial animals were divided precisely in half lengthwise and laid upon the ground. Then the two people involved walked between the divided parts. God established a covenant with Abram this way (Genesis 15:7-21).

We have already mentioned the significance of eating covenant meals, especially bread and salt. Sometimes outer garments and weapons were exchanged with the promise to look after the covenant partner's life and interests as though they were one's own. Even the saying, "Blood is thicker than water," comes from the Hebrew concept of covenants. The idea was that the *blood* of the covenant superseded all other loyalties, even those relating to the birth *water*.

The marriage covenant was sealed with a cup of wine. Wine represented blood (Matthew 26:27-28) [hence its suitability for covenant making], sacrifice, and also joy. These three elements were intrinsic to the marriage relationship.

After all the negotiation and talk, a bride price settled, a gift having been offered, the man would then pour a cup of wine for the woman and place it before her. Now came the suspenseful part....At this point, the woman had about thirty seconds to make up her mind. If she did *not* drink, the man left and never came again. If the woman was willing to receive the man and his proposed condition, she would accept his gift and also drink the cup of wine which sealed the covenant. This showed that she was willing to take his name upon her.

This act had to be witnessed by two observers in the room who were unrelated to the man or the woman. Technically, once the above conditions were met, they were considered married. If her bridegroom should die before the marriage was consummated, she would be called a "virgin who is a widow" and considered to have a very special kind of sadness, because she had all of the promises and none of the fulfillment of marriage.

Following the woman's acceptance, the groom and sometimes the girl's father recited additional formal statements. The father-in-law said, "Thou shalt this day be my son-in-law." To the bride, the groom would speak the words, "Thou art *set apart* (or consecrated) for me according to the law of Moses and Israel." Interestingly, the same word for "set apart," in New Testament Greek "*hagiazo*," was also used to describe the state of a temple once it was dedicated (Peterson 73).

You will notice that this particular way of betrothal and marriage does not require a rabbi or a priest, only a man, a woman, and two witnesses. The two witnesses were required to oversee the signing of the *ketubah* and the giving of the gift. They listened to the pronouncement of the bridegroom's ritual statements and witnessed the bride's acceptance by drinking the cup of wine. By their witness, the marriage agreement was "made sure" (Freeman 25).

The bride from this point on would wear a veil over her hair whenever she was in public. This would indicate her status as a betrothed woman and signal that she was not available to anyone else. She was now called a *me'kudeshet*, meaning one who is betrothed, sanctified and dedicated to another. For the rest of her life, her headdress would symbolize her faithfulness to her husband (Stern 474).

Properly understood, her veil hid only that which was too precious for the common, careless gaze. To be veiled was not considered an indication of oppression or inferiority. Since her hair also represented glory, it was to be enjoyed exclusively by her groom. In fact, only those things which were treasured and glorious were veiled. One example was when Moses stood before the children of Israel to address them after his encounter with the Lord. When he returned to the people, Moses then had to veil his face because it was so filled with glory that the people were frightened (Exodus 34:29-35). Additionally, the largest veil in the Israelite temple was to conceal the Holy of Holies from those who were not prepared or qualified to enter. Like a temple, the woman was now "set apart" for holiness—the greatest holiness of all—

which was to eventually bring forth new life.

Another designation she now had was "a garden enclosed." Only her husband was rightfully entitled to enjoy the beauty and fruit of that garden.

The betrothal was usually followed by a feast at the bride's home. But custom required that once this process was completed, the relationship accepted, witnessed, and sealed, the bridegroom would then have to leave his bride. He would go to his father's house to prepare a place for her.

CHAPTER FOUR

Preparing a Place

The newly engaged bridegroom was now a "man with a mission." He would return to his father's household and begin building a new *bet hatanut* or wedding chamber for himself and his new bride (Collins 106). Scholars have determined that at the time of Christ a common household arrangement around Capernaum and Korazin was an *insula*. An insula consisted of many separate but adjacent houses–residences for various family members–which were built around a central courtyard (Mackie 91).

Insula

It was a family compound where servants lived with the families as members of the household. The father's house served as the hub or focal point of the entire community. This arrangement was very supportive in terms of caring for the needs of the children and the elderly by the entire extended family.

By building his own "little mansion" or bridal chamber for their honeymoon in this area, the groom and his bride were recognized and assimilated into the family circle as full adults. Zola Levitt, a Hebrew Christian, in his book *A Christian Love Story* says:

We should appreciate that this was a complex undertaking for the bridegroom. He would actually build a separate building on his father's property, or decorate a room in his father's house. The bridal chamber had to be beautiful—one doesn't honeymoon just anywhere; and it had to be stocked with provisions since the bride and groom were going to remain inside for seven days. This construction project would ordinarily take the better part of a year (3).

During this period of preparation, the betrothed man was exempted from military service, lest anything happen that might prevent him from returning to take his bride. This law is given in Deuteronomy 20:7:

> *And what man is there that hath betrothed a wife, and hath not taken her? Let him go and return unto his house, lest he die in the battle and another man take her.*

Nothing took precedence over the importance of establishing a new home and family.

While the new home was under construction, the newly engaged couple did not see each other. If they needed to communicate, it was done by means of the "friend of the bridegroom," who carried messages between them during the betrothal period (Freeman 423).

The new home was built under the direct personal supervision of the groom's father. In that culture, a son is considered to be a representative of his father, and everything that the son does reflects either favorably or unfavorably on the father. Every aspect of the son's daily life was considered an extension of his father's training and teachings. Jewish writings plainly express this understanding:

> If a young man was well-versed in Bible study and was on good terms with his fellow men, it was said of him, *"Happy his father* who taught him the Law. See how well-mannered and proper are his actions."

But if the son studied the Law and yet was not honest in his dealings or on good terms with his fellow men, it was said, "*Pity his father* who taught him the Law, see how corrupt his deeds and how ugly his behavior!" (Yoma 86a—Leibowitz 69)

With such close identification between a father and his son, the father wanted everything regarding the bride's new home to be as beautiful and perfect as it could be. The quality of the workmanship portrayed the quality of the father's instructions and was a visual representation of the groom's love and caring for his bride.

The young man would work long hours, eager to finish the dwelling so that he could return and take his bride to their new home. The father of the groom was the sole judge of when the preparations were complete. It seems logical to assume that if it were only up to the young man, he would throw up some quick lean-to and hurry to get his bride. But his father was less emotionally involved and would be more concerned with quality craftsmanship. When the father determined everything was ready, he gave permission for the son to claim his bride. No one knew when that permission was forthcoming, so not even the bride and groom knew the exact day of the wedding. Only the father knew.

Meanwhile, the bride was also busy making preparations for her future and the new life she would share with her husband. There was wedding clothing to prepare, including much elaborate colorful embroidery. Swaddling bands were also to be embroidered with symbols indicating family history and genealogy. According to ancient and modern custom, the embroidery, to be acceptable, must be exactly the same on both sides. This was a type showing that the outward life and the inner life were the same—they were never to have a "wrong side" to their character. Under the wedding canopy, these decorated bands would be tied around the clasped right hands on the bride and groom; hence the saying, "They tied the knot." These bands would later be used to fasten the swaddling clothes of their children.

The young girl would also learn and refine her homemaking skills–tasks which required resourcefulness and diligent effort. Women drew water and carried it into the house (1 Samuel 9:11-13), ground the grain into flour using a large flat stone (*quern*) and a small grindstone held in the hands, baked the bread (1 Samuel 8:13), boiled porridge and other dishes, and were responsible for the storage of food resources–grain, wine, oil, and condiments –and their allocation as well. They spun, wove, and sewed, and they may have shared in making pottery. They must also have expended much energy caring for gardens and domestic animals. As an analogy, it is useful to recall the hard labor done by women in the pioneer settlements during the American colonial period (Holladay 296).

Providing the oil was also a woman's duty, a duty held to be symbolic; and she particularly had to take care of the very pure oil for the Sabbath lamp, which she was to tend so that it would not go out on the holy day (Daniel-Rops 129).

In addition to these important skills, the bride's personal preparation was also considered. She adorned herself with the gifts that her bridegroom had given her, desiring that they would enhance her beauty in his eyes. She practiced the application of her wedding make-up and paid special attention to her fingernails, hair, and skin so that she would be as attractive as possible for her new husband. The ideal complexion was smooth, glossy, and shining. This is reflected in the words of David "that our daughters may be as corner stones, polished after the similitude of a palace" (Psalms 144:12).

Before the wedding, the new bride would have a ritual bath or immersion at a *mikvah*. The term for *mikvah* is actually identical to the word used in Genesis 1:10 to describe the primeval "gathering of the waters" (Frankel 187). For this reason, the *mikvah* was a pool that was filled from a natural water source –such as a spring, lake, or stream–these sources were considered to be "living water." If such a source was unavailable, an artificial pool containing undrawn freely flowing rain or spring water was acceptable. The *mikvah* had to be large enough to immerse oneself completely. The idea of using only pure "living water" for immersion was important, because:

> ...the root word for immersion means "to dip, soak, immerse" into a liquid, so that what is dipped takes on the qualities of what it has been dipped in—for example, cloth in dye or leather in a tanning solution. (Stern 15)

The bride, of course, would desire to have the same qualities of cleanliness and purity as those represented by the waters of the *mikvah*. Her life and body were to be the gift of a living sacrifice to her husband, and to be pure without any spot or blemish was a condition required of sacrifices (Ephesians 5:27; Romans 12:1).

A modern Jewish rabbi has written about the meaning of the word "sacrifice":

> The Hebrew word for "sacrifice" *(korban le-hakriv)* is from the root meaning as "to come near, to approach...to become closely involved in a relationship with someone."
> ...Unfortunately, no word in the English language can adequately render the idea behind the Hebrew word *korban*. We use the word "sacrifice" for lack of a better word. The idea of sacrifice or offering seems to indicate a gift or present; giving up something of value yourself, for the benefit of another. None of this gift-giving idea, however, is present in the idea of the *korban*. First of all, it is a word which never carries a connotation of a present or gift; it is used by the Bible in the context of man's relationship with God. Thus its true meaning can only be grasped through its root...the concept of coming close (Richman 7).

The Jewish bride did not immerse herself because of uncleanness, but in preparation for holiness, to fulfill God's commandment to be fruitful and multiply. The groom, while not required to do so, generally chose to participate in a *mikvah* in preparation for his coming marriage. In this act, the waters also represented the waters in the garden of Eden bringing back the purity of the relationship between the man, the woman, and God. On their wedding day, after fasting and repentance, the couple were declared free from sin (Flaugher 31).

After her immersion in the *mikvah*, the bride's friends would help her anoint herself as part of the preparation for marriage. Middle Eastern people used fragrant oils to protect and heal their bodies and to make themselves pleasant to others. A bride especially would take care to wear fragrant perfume that would make her "nice to be near" (Wiersbe 41).

In ancient times, before a new bride was to be presented to a king, she underwent a year of purification and preparation. We can read an example of this in Esther 2:12.

> *Now when every maid's turn was come to go in to king Ahasuerus, after that she had been twelve months, according to the manner of the women, (for so were the days of their purifications accomplished, to wit, six months with oil of myrrh, and six months with sweet odours, and with other things for the purifying of the women)...*

Anciently, myrrh was used for four purposes: anointing oil, perfume, ceremonial cleansing, and burial preparation. Myrrh means "bitterness" and was associated with purification because it typified repentance and cleanliness. Every bride would desire to be as clean and as sweet as possible in preparation for her new role.

From the time of the bridegroom's departure until he returned for her a year or so later, the bride placed a lamp in her window and kept it continually burning every night. It was a token of her faithfulness, and she lived for the day her beloved would return for her. The focus of her life revolved around the thoughts of her future happiness with her new husband. She kept her *ketuba* near, and its promises would reassure her that her waiting would not be in vain. Having paid such a high price for her, he would surely return.

As the time of the wedding drew closer, the young girl anxiously awaited her groom's arrival. By custom, it would be sudden, with an element of surprise (the Jews thought this was romantic), and often late at night. She invited her sisters, cousins, and friends to join her vigil and be supportive at this time of joyous anticipation. They passed the evening, discussing family matters, complimenting the bride on her appearance, and they also sang songs and encouraged each other during the wait. Night after night, they would strain to hear the shouts of the bridegroom and his friends. The long wait and each temporary disappointment caused greatly heightened emotion and increased already intense desire.

The young bride would have gathered all the things she needed to take with her, including the traditional gift for the groom, which was a *tallit* or prayer shawl.

Tallit

As a note of interest, it was customary for a man to begin wearing a *tallit* on the day he was married, and he would do so every day thereafter until the day he died. It would be worn at temple and synagogue services and every time he prayed. There was a special meaning in the bride's giving of the *tallit*. A *tallit* has a total of four tassels with eight strings in each tassel, equaling thirty-two strings. The number 32 in Hebrew has the same numerical value as the word "*lev*," meaning "heart." The bride was giving her "heart" to her husband, which he would wear for all to see (Blech 99).

The bride would also have her honeymoon clothes packed, and her wedding dress ready. She had already experienced the ritual immersion that prepared her for the beautiful assignment to bring forth children. Of course, she was careful during the waiting period to keep herself clean and well groomed and her clothing unsoiled and well cared for. It would be a horrible situation to have her bridegroom come and find her unprepared. The bridegroom would feel deeply hurt and insulted to think that his bride felt that he wasn't worth the trouble and care it took to be ready and waiting for him. It was certain that, as time passed and the messages were relayed from the groom through his special friend indicating the preparations were nearly complete, she watched for him virtually on a hourly basis.

Finally the great day came when the "wedding house" was finished and the father gave his long awaited permission. While the groom called and gathered his friends, the father sent servants with the *second* announcement that the wedding feasting and festivities were about to start. The first invitation or *calling* had been sent earlier when the betrothal began. This first invitation was serious and acceptance of it implied a firm commitment to attend. Anciently, two invitations were always given. Examples are found in Esther 5:8 and 6:14. In Jerusalem, according to Judah Nadich, if you planned to accept an invitation to attend a banquet, you made it known to others. In his book, *Jewish Legends of the Second Commonwealth*, he relates the following:

> No [citizen of Jerusalem] would attend a banquet without changing his buckle from the right to the left shoulder. For what reason? So that another person should not extend to him an invitation that would be wasted. (Yerushalmi Avodah Zarah 39C)

A double invitation was vital in determining the plans for the wedding feast. An example of this double invitation is also shown in Luke 14:16-17. [*Bracketed words mine*]

> ...a certain man made [planned] a great supper [banquet, usually a wedding feast] and bade [invited, called the first time] many: and sent his servant at suppertime [feast was now ready] to say to them that were bidden, [those invited the first time who had accepted the invitation] come; [the second invitation and announcement] for all things are now ready.

Kenneth Bailey explains the reason for the double invitation:

> A host sends out his invitations and receives acceptance. The meat will be killed and cooked based on the number of guests...one or two chickens (2-4 guests), or a duck (5-8 guests), or a kid (10-15 acceptances), or a sheep (if there are 15-35 people), or a calf (35-75)... Once the countdown starts it cannot be stopped. The appropriate animal is killed and must be eaten that night. The guests who accept invitations are duty-bound to appear. Then at the "hour of the banquet," a servant is sent out with the traditional message, "Come! all is now ready," meaning the meat is cooked and we are ready for you (*Through Peasant Eyes* 94-95).

The present imperative "Come!" means literally "continue coming." The guests began their action by accepting the invitation. They continued it by responding to the messenger. The initial acceptance obliged the guest to respond to the summons at the "hour of the banquet" (Bailey 95). Only those who accepted the first invitation would receive the final invitation when the feast was ready.

While the father did his part, the groom prepared carefully for the home-taking of his bride. He dressed in his richest garments, sometimes wearing a golden crown. His garments would be scented with frankincense and myrrh, and his sash would be of brilliantly colored silk. Although the bride would be beautifully adorned, the groom was the center of attention (Nelson 435). The scriptures focused not on the bride, but on the bridegroom as being happy and radiant on the wedding day

42 / PREPARING A PLACE

(Psalms 19:5). His companions would also wear their very best for this important occasion.

Since every marriage worked for the perpetuation of Israel, they were celebrated with enthusiasm as a religious and patriotic duty. Therefore, great importance was lent to the wedding procession that wound its merry way through the streets. A well-known tradition says that in the First Temple, built by King Solomon, there was a special Gate of the Bridegroom. There the people of the city would gather to watch wedding processions enter and depart. When the groom appeared, they directed to him the customary blessing for offspring: "May God, whose throne is set in this house, rejoice your heart with sons and daughters!" (Ausubel 488).

The "taking" of a bride was a very joyful occasion. There was much singing, dancing, and merriment. The bridegroom, his best friend and the other friends who were attendants, set off in a noisy procession carrying torches and blowing on trumps, or *shofars*. Anyone who desired to join the group was welcome, and all students would be excused from their studies to participate.

Shofar

When nearing the bride's home, a messenger was sent ahead to give the shout, "The bridegroom cometh!" (This was when the foolish virgins went to get oil [Matthew 25:10].) They would allow a short time (never more than half an hour) to give the bride time to make final preparations and then they would call out again, "The bridegroom cometh!" Following the shout, the group would rush to the bride's house. The groom would charge in, and after the father made sure that he was the man with the contract, the father would stand aside and let the groom "take"

the bride. Because of the mix-up with Jacob getting the wrong bride the first time, a rule was made in Jewish marriage law that the groom had the right to veil the bride at her house so he could make sure that it was the correct girl, and he was not being tricked. The veil was left in place during the procession and for most of the wedding ceremony. Its removal was a significant event.

Leave-taking was a tender moment for the bride and her family, because it was the final surrender of her former name and clan and symbolized her new patriarchal loyalties. In a real way, when she went out the door of her parent's home escorted by her husband, her new life began. It was now time for the procession back to the father's house. This began the second part of the marriage ceremony called *nissu'in*.

Nissu'in is derived from the root word *nasu*, which means: "to carry," "to bear," or "to lift up." The bride was lifted into a special chair called an *aperion* and carried to her new home. The four strong men who bore the *aperion* were given the honorary title, *Giborei Yisrael*, or heroes of Israel (Lash 26).

Aperion

A description of what followed is found in I Maccabees 9:39 :

> There was much ado and great carriage; and the bridegroom came forth, and his friends and brethren, to meet them with drums, and instruments of music, and many weapons.

This time was also called "the bringing of the lamp," meaning the bride. While going to the groom's home, the bride wore her hair loose and flowing as a token of virginity. Later at her new home, some of the women would have the task of beautifully arranging the bride's hair. Her locks were often braided with gold, pearls, and precious jewels.

The wedding festivities, and especially her adornments, would always be remembered by the bride. The prophet Jeremiah made reference to this thought, "Can a maid forget her ornaments, or a bride her attire?" (Jeremiah 2:32) The apostle John saw New Jerusalem "prepared as a bride adorned for her husband" (Revelations 21:2) (Mackie 131).

The procession included the attendants of the bride and groom and other guests invited to the wedding. Some of her relatives preceded her in the procession, accompanied by musicians, singers, and dancers. Those in the procession scattered parched ears of grain to the children along the way. Wine, oil, and nuts were also freely distributed to the adults (Edersheim L&T 254). A hen and rooster were carried before the bride and the groom in the procession as a fertility symbol. Later, upon the conclusion of the nuptial rite, these were sent flying over the wedding chamber with a cluck and a cackle (Ausubel 489).

The most important period of the marriage festivities was when the bride entered her new home. The bride and groom were sometimes crowned with real crowns or with garlands of roses, myrtle, or olive leaves. (This lovely custom was discontinued after the last temple was destroyed in 70 A.D. in deference to the sorrow the nation of Israel felt. Olive garlands were a symbol of great joy, and such joy was inappropriate in view of the temple's destruction.) The couple was treated like royalty during this time. The new husband was literally considered a king and priest in his own home, with his wife as queen (Mackie 123). The Psalmist must have pictured this important moment and compared it to the marriage of a king:

> *She shall be brought unto the king in raiment of needlework: the virgins her companions that follow her*

> *shall be brought unto thee. With gladness and rejoicing shall they be brought; they shall enter into the king's palace* (Psalms 45:14-15).

Daniel-Rops tells us a bit more concerning this critical element in the Jewish wedding when the bride and groom reached the wedding house.

> So the procession reached the bridegroom's house. His parents then uttered a traditional blessing which was taken up by all of those present and which expressed their wishes for the happiness and fruitfulness of the marriage. There were several of these blessings in the scriptures—such as Genesis 24:60 and Ruth 4:11—and the people were expected to know them (124).

After these blessings were recited, the bride and groom and all of the invited guests who carried their lights went in. The door was then shut and bolted because there was not enough room for all who would seek to enter. Even the invited guests who came late were left outside. To be late was unthinkable at such an important occasion and was considered a gross insult to the host. The heavy barred door could only be opened with difficulty, and servants were instructed to refuse entry to latecomers.

For those not prepared or on time for the marriage and wedding feast, there was great disappointment. The bitter truth of the Jewish proverb, "A door that is shut is not easily opened," became a stark reality.

CHAPTER FIVE

The Ten Bridesmaids

In the parable of the ten virgins, Christ tells of a bridegroom who returns to take his bride. The bride and her attendants are expecting his return, but of course, the exact time and day were not known. This story is told in Matthew 25:1-13. Most of the bracketed words are from the Jewish New Testament to add clarity.

> *Then shall the kingdom of heaven be likened unto ten virgins, which took their lamps and went forth to meet the bridegroom. [Wait for him at the bride's home.] And five of them were wise, and five were foolish. They that were foolish took [only] their lamps and took no [extra] oil with them. But the wise took [additional] oil in their vessels [along] with their lamps. While the bridegroom tarried, [was late] they all slumbered and slept. At midnight, there was a cry made, [someone shouted] "Behold, the bridegroom cometh; go ye out to meet him."*
>
> *Then all those virgins arose [the girls all woke up] and trimmed their lamps [prepared their lamps for lighting]. And the foolish said unto the wise, "Give us of your oil; for our lamps are gone out." But the wise answered, saying, "Not so; lest there be not enough for us and you; but go ye rather to them that sell [the oil dealers], and buy for yourselves." And while they went to buy, the bridegroom came, and they that were ready went in with him to the marriage: and the door was shut. Afterward came also the other [foolish] virgins, saying, "Lord, Lord, open to us." But he answered and said, "Verily I say unto you, I know you not."*

It is enlightening to think about some of the elements in this parable. In the story there were ten virgins, or bridesmaids, as we would call them. Ten is a very significant number to the Jews.

According to some sources, ten was the minimum number of lamps that were required at a wedding while the traditional blessings were recited.

It was also considered a religious duty to bring light when attending a wedding. Light was associated with marriage as a special metaphor for joy, and, during the entire wedding celebration, the father's house was continually lit for the seven-day period. There is a marriage parable in the Hasidic literature, attributed to Baal Shem Tov which shows an additional facet of how light relates to marriage.

> From every human being there rises a light that reaches straight to heaven. And when two that are destined for each other find one another, their streams of light flow together forming a single brighter light from their united being (cited in Flaugher 14).

Most weddings took place in early autumn when people were finished with the harvest and had extra time to participate in extended wedding festivities. During that season, days were short, and the wedding party began in the early evening and continued all night. The oil lamps and candles were their only light source.

The candles and olive oil (or liquefied butter) for the lamps were prepared before the wedding took place. A pinch of salt was added to the oil to make the flame brighter. Since light was a symbol of happiness, no wedding was properly conducted without the greatest amount possible. To bring a lamp to the festivities was also a responsibility that every guest had as his personal contribution to the joy of the event. Men and women dancers would often hold lamps in their hands, and sometimes men would fasten candles to their daggers.

Visitors generally purchased oil in the town where the wedding was to take place. Some people, however, because they feared being unable to obtain oil and candles, brought their own supplies with them. As the bride was escorted during the evening, and because the hour of their coming was not exactly known, those unprepared–to their great disappointment–found the stores closed and the oil venders themselves waiting for the coming bridal party (*Gospel Light,* Lamsa 140).

There are interesting associations with light and darkness in the Jewish mind, and these shed understanding on some sayings in the scriptures. First, for some background, a native in Bible lands would never sleep in a dark room. However poor he was, he had to have some small light in the house. To those people, light represented a triumph of good over evil, light over darkness, and literally, the supremacy of life over death. A Middle Eastern home was never in darkness, except for one of two reasons: either someone living there died, or the house was deserted.

There are many references to lights and lamps in the scriptures and at times they are symbolic of the continuation of the family. Even one of the names for Heavenly Father is "The Father of Lights."

> *Every good gift, and every perfect gift is from above, and cometh down from the Father of lights, with whom is no variableness, neither shadow of turning* (James 1:17).

Job 18:5-6 says:

> ...*the light of the wicked shall be put out, and the spark of his fire shall not shine. The light shall be dark in his tabernacle, and his candle shall be put out with him.*

In Proverbs 13:9 we read:

> *The light of the righteous rejoiceth; but the lamp of the wicked shall be put out.*

2 Samuel 14:7 continues:

> ...*and so they shall quench my coal which is left [the only burning coal I have], and shall not leave to my husband neither name nor remainder upon the earth.*

If a woman's son was killed, her "spark of life" and "light" would be extinguished, and her husband's family line would be "put out." So light, in this context, can mean having an heir to carry on the family line.

They were also very superstitious about light. Since ancient banquets were held at night in rooms that were very well-lit, anyone who was excluded from a special feast was said to be "cast out of the lighted room into the outer darkness of night." In the teachings of Jesus, this kind of exclusion is likened to the day of judgment. In Matthew 8:12 we read:

> ...*the children of the kingdom shall be cast out into* outer darkness.

Matthew 22:13 and 25:30 repeat the theme:

> *Bind him, hand and foot, and take him away, and cast him into* outer darkness.

> *And cast ye the unprofitable servant into* outer darkness; *there shall be weeping and gnashing of teeth.*

The expression "outer darkness" takes on a new meaning when we realize that in addition to having a great dread of darkness, those not attending to the wedding feast would also suffer the agony of being alone when everyone else was rejoicing together. Israelites were are very sociable people and this would have been extremely painful. The Savior could not have chosen more appropriate words than "outer darkness" to represent the future punishment of the unrighteous (Wight 63).

It is interesting to note that generally in the Middle East, doors were left open all day as a sign of hospitality. But with approaching darkness, the doors were always bolted. Some helpful information is found in *Bible Manners and Customs*:

The door is a place of peculiar sanctity and importance. The difference between the outside and the inside is that of two different worlds. In large houses the door-keeper sits at the entrance to answer inquiries and conduct visitors within, and at night he sleeps in a small room within the entrance at the side of the door, keeping guard over the premises. He is charged with the protection of the family without being included in its membership. This position of menial servant and door-keeper is alluded to in Psalms 84:10. In smaller homes, a servant or family member calls out, "Who is it?" If the visitor be a well-known friend, he exclaims,"It is I!" or "Open." The recognized tone of the voice is sufficient—no name is given (Mackie 95).

When knocking at a door, an individual did not give his name, because it was felt that an impostor or thief might try to gain access by using the name of a family friend. His *voice* had to be recognized. This was a well-known custom anciently. There wasn't any spite on the part of the bridegroom or his father (See also Matthew 7:21-23). So, in the parable of the foolish virgins, when the Lord says, "I know you not," he is saying that he does not recognize the virgins' voices. There hadn't been enough geniune interaction that their voices would be familiar. Their pleas would go unheeded.

Other commentaries are also helpful in shedding light on this parable. Craig Keener reports:

> The foolish bride's maids missed the entire procession back to the groom's house along with the festive singing and dancing that attended that procession. They also missed the critical element of the Jewish wedding in which the bride was brought into the groom's home....Having insulted the dignity of the host, they were not admitted to the feast which lasted for seven days following the ceremony (Keener 117).

CHAPTER SIX

The Wedding Canopy

Upon entry into the father's house, each guest had his feet and hands washed by servants with pure water that was kept in stone jars for this exclusive purpose. Then each guest was anointed, embraced, and kissed. In Hebrew culture, such kisses and embraces were signs of reconciliation and restorations of friendship in case there had been any bad feelings between them. Marriages were a time when good feelings were felt by everyone involved. These customs are referenced in Luke 7:44-46, where the man who invited Christ to dinner neglected every one of them. Their omission was very demeaning, especially in a culture where an invitation to eat implied affection, intimacy, and mutual confidence.

Another Jewish custom was to wear a "wedding garment" when attending a wedding. To wear one's very best and most beautiful clothing was an indication of esteem for the host as well as for the bridal pair.

If the groom's father was a king, this wedding garment was often given as a gift to the guests. White was a color associated with royalty, and white mantles or robes were especially valued gifts. Extensive wardrobes were a part of Middle Eastern wealth, and it was a special mark of honor to receive such a garment from a king.

In Matthew 22:11 it says, "And when the king came in to see the guests, he saw there a man which had not on the wedding garment." It was customary for monarchs who gave magnificent banquets to come in and see the guests after they were assembled. Each guest was individually greeted. Allusion is made to this custom in the above text and also in Luke 14:10: "When he who bade (invited) thee cometh." The context plainly indicates that the guests had assembled before the host made his appearance. In the parable, although most of the guests were from the poorer classes who had been called suddenly, the king manifested surprise at finding one of them without a suitable wedding garment. This was an indication that kingly generosity had been disdained by an invited guest.

Of course, anyone who chose to offend his noble host by refusing the offered gift of suitable attire was cast out. To have acceptable garments and your own light insured the right to stay and enjoy the wedding feast.

It is instructive to consider that in the scriptures, *charity*–the "pure love of Christ"–is described as "the greatest of all the gifts" (Moroni 7:46-48) and compared to a covering like a mantle (D&C 88:125). Perhaps it fits the type of the required wedding garment.

After each guest was greeted, an event known as *Kabbalat Panim* took place. In Hebrew, this expression means "meeting of the faces." It was a time for all of the guests to greet one another and get acquainted or renew old friendships. Some of the faces were very familiar and some were being met for the first time. It was often a joyous reunion with loved ones and with extended family, friends, and neighbors (Flaugher 64).

While the *Kabbalat Panim* was being enjoyed, the bride and groom were dressed in their wedding clothing. The bride, who had already had her *mikvah* was again anointed with sweet-smelling olive oil, symbolizing her joy, and then she was dressed in her white wedding dress. In some areas, her veil would be trimmed with beautiful needlework of scarlet and gold.

White was also traditional for the clothing worn by the groom. In Judaism, white clothing did not denote virginity, but rather purity from sin. It also was a similitude for the dignity and glory of God and symbolized a change of status and new privileges (See Zechariah 3:3-5). Remember that each groom at the time of his wedding and later in his own home was to be considered as a king and a priest. (I am indebted to Nehama Leibowitz and Charles W. Slemming for many insights and extensive treatments regarding the spiritual significance of the Old Testament temple clothing and wedding clothing.)

There are scriptures which are helpful in understanding the wedding clothing and their metaphorical extensions to righteous behavior. In Ecclesiastes 9:8 it says,

> Let thy garments be always white and let thy head lack no ointment.

The Hebrew translations of this verse gives *white garments* the connotations of *purity* and *cleanliness*; and the ointment mentioned was a synonym for anointing oil. Originally, kings were anointed with oil (primarily made from pressed olives) before receiving their crown. The anointing symbolized joy, honor, favor, and long life.

The white clothing had both religious and royal associations. Kings in the Old Testament wore fine white linen—similar in texture to modern damask with a silky feel. The best of these materials came from Egypt. The robes from this material were also called "garments of splendor and beauty."

Priests who served in the temple also wore garments of fine white linen during their ministrations. These garments came from the weaver seamless, bound at the waist with a girdle, decorated by needlework. The priest's robe nearly covered the feet and was skillfully woven (like damask) in a diamond or chessboard pattern (Nelson 488). This special clothing was worn to distinguish between the sacred and the everyday, and it was a reminder to assist them in their task to become holy. It was thought that donning a white garment symbolized man's vesting himself with good moral qualities.

Therefore, the groom's wedding clothing was very helpful in reminding him of his role and responsibilities as a new husband and father-to-be. His main article of clothing was a *kittel*, which was a white coat or tunic girded with a white sash. (The word "coat" in Hebrew is *"kethoneth,"* meaning "to cover" or "to hide." It is the same word used in Genesis 3:21.) This coat was associated with purity, forgiveness of sins, and solemn joy. The white color and simple design were thought to eliminate distinctions between the rich and the poor (Frankel 92). The white sash was a symbol of service, since sashes were used to gird loins, and girded loins denoted alertness, strength, and readiness for action. The groom also wore a miter or linen cap on his head, a headdress similar to that worn by the priests in the temple (Flaugher 32).

Isaiah 61:10 describes some of these customs:

> *I delight greatly in my Lord; my soul rejoices in my God. For he has clothed me with garments of salvation and arrayed me in a robe of righteousness, as a* bridegroom *adorns his head like a* priest *and a bride adorns herself with her jewels* (NIV).

It was thought that this white cap was a symbol of being crowned with holiness and righteousness. Since the head denotes authority, wisdom, and experience, the white miter also represented the wisdom that comes with age.

Two scriptures that reflect this understanding are Proverbs 16:31 and Daniel 7:9. In Proverbs it says:

> *The hoary* (white) *head is a crown of glory, if it be found in the way of righteousness.*

Daniel continues the metaphor:

> *I beheld until the thrones were cast down, and the Ancient of Days did sit, whose garment was white as snow, and the hair of his head was like the pure wool* (white)...

The word for this special cap (Strong 4021) is derived from a word which means "to elevate" or "to lift up," signifying the honor due to this new head of a household in Israel.

One Jewish commentator, Benno Jacob (Leibowitz 529) taught that this special clothing represented a restoration of the garment of light that was lost in the Garden of Eden. By the act of clothing Adam and Eve, God was consecrating them to be parents. There is much in Jewish thought connecting the new bridal pair to the very first married couple in the Garden of Eden. This will be considered in greater detail later in this chapter when the seven wedding benedictions are mentioned.

The marriage *huppah* (or canopy) had several associations. It was the chamber or "wedding house," the bridal canopy, or the term for the marriage ceremony itself. Today, only the latter two meanings apply (Frankel 77). The canopy is understood as a sign of God's presence, and the word *huppah* means "that which covers or floats above." To the Jew, it recalls the tent of Abraham, which had doors on all four sides, so that visitors were always welcome. It represented a number of important concepts:

1. the house of the bridegroom to which he welcomes the bride;
2. the tabernacle in the wilderness where God and Israel began their life together;
3. the divine light that surrounds all creation;
4. the covering of God over the couple to be married;
5. the bridal chamber where the consummation of the wedding took place;
6. a portal or gateway, symbolizing the bridal couple's entrance into the covenant of marriage and accompanying emotional, physical and spiritual transitions (Flaugher 34).

Canopy

The canopy was often set up outside, sometimes on the flat roof of the home under the stars, recalling the promise to Abraham of numerous posterity. Sometimes it was a large *tallit* which symbolized God's sheltering love over the new couple. The poles were made from branches cut from trees planted at the time of the birth of the bride and groom. It was the custom to plant a cedar tree at the birth of a son. Cedar wood was used in the temple and cedars bear cones in very old age. The custom for daughters was to plant pine or cypress trees. There was a tradition that Noah's ark was made from cypress wood (a.k.a. gopher wood) and the ark was a feminine symbol. Both pine and cypress trees were highly valued for their oil. All of the trees were evergreen and symbolized beauty and longevity for that culture.

There are no complete descriptions of covenant weddings in the Bible. We must take hints from the text and also from traditional Jewish sources to flesh out this most important ceremony. The following is a composite description and general consensus. The symbolic teachings are helpful in understanding some allusions in scriptures, since wedding traditions were based on scriptures.

1. The groom was escorted to the canopy by his parents. It represented his house, and he would welcome her under its covering. The ritual statement, "Blessed be he who comes," was repeated as the groom proceeded to the *huppah*. "Blessed be he who comes" is an idiomatic expression which means "welcome" (Chumey 125).
2. The bride was then led to the canopy by her parents.
3. The officiator then faced the couple and read the Psalm of Thanksgiving (Psalm 100).
4. A goblet of wine was raised, and a blessing was said over the wine. This was called "The Cup of Joy." Both bride and groom drank from the same cup, indicating they would share the joys of life together.
5. A very old tradition has the bride circling the groom seven times at this point. This is referencing a scrip-

ture in Jeremiah where it says that "a woman shall compass a man" (Jeremiah 31:22).

6. A ring was then placed on the right index finger of the bride's hand. The right hand was used for making covenants, eating, and reading the scriptures with a *yad* (a pointer shaped like a right hand with index finger extended). The left hand was never used except for base needs. It was extremely offensive to even wave at someone with the left hand, much less to make a covenant with it. The ring used for this ceremony was often owned by the community and used at all weddings.

Community Ring

The house depicted on the ring represented the new household being established and later reflected the desire that each righteous home would hasten the restoration of the Temple for all Israel.

7. The groom then lifted the bride's veil and placed the corner of it on his shoulder. This was a proclamation to everyone present that the government of his bride now rested on his shoulder. This is wonderfully alluded to in Isaiah 9:6 where it says, "...the government shall be upon his shoulder...," portraying the Messiah as a type of the Bridegroom.

Anciently, the shoulder was where large keys were carried, and also the priest's portion in the Temple was the right shoulder of the sacrificial animal.

58 / THE WEDDING CANOPY

Man Carrying Wooden Keys

Since the shoulder and the arm were connected, it also symbolized power to act with authority. According to Vine's topical index (23) the shoulder also denoted strength. After placing her veil on his shoulder, the groom wrapped his *tallit* around his bride. This was also called "covering with the skirt" or "spreading the corner of the garment." It implied protection of a conjugal nature. (This is also alluded to in Ruth 3:9, Freeman-Chadwick 202.)

8. The *ketuba* or marriage contract was read aloud in the presence of two special witnesses and all the guests.

9. The *Sheva Berachot* (Seven Bridal Blessings) were then recited by the men only. This is in keeping with the story of Ruth, where Boaz took ten elders of the city and had them witness the proceedings as he made the offer to redeem the field of Naomi and to thus take Ruth as his wife because he was a near kinsman (See Ruth 4:2). After witnessing the redemption, the ten elders then blessed Ruth saying,

"The Lord make the woman who is come into your house like Rachel and like Leah, which two did build the house of Israel, and do worthily in Ephrathah and be famous in Bethlehem" (Ruth 4:11) [As an aside, there is an ancient tradition that the fields redeemed by Boaz may well have been the fields where the shepherds were visited by angels at the time of Jesus Christ's birth (Flaugher 37)]. There is some variation in the wording of the blessings, but generally they follow the context below. The person pronouncing the blessings raises a cup of wine and gives thanks to God:

A. for *the fruit of the vine*–literally, the wine, symbol of rejoicing and figuratively for the future children of the couple (the "vine" is a symbol for "wife") who will also bring joy and rejoicing to the new family.
B. for *creating the universe*–for the bride and groom, marriage typifies the renewal of the world.
C. for *the creation of mankind* (literally *the Adam* in Hebrew)–this introduces the theme of the ancient paradise, signifying that the bridal couple is on this day reborn, as it were.
D. for *creating human beings in His image, in such fashion that they can in turn create life*– this recognized God's influence in uniting the bridal pair in marriage.
E. for *His grace, that he will make Zion joyful again through the return of her children*–the hope that Zion will be restored takes precedence over individual joy.
F. for *making the groom and bride joyful and bringing gladness to them as He did to the first*

> man and woman in the Garden of Eden—each
> new marriage is a type of the first marriage
> in Eden.
>
> G. for Him who created joy and gladness, bride and
> groom, mirth, song, delight, rejoicing, love,
> harmony, peace, and companionship—God is
> implored to restore speedily to the cities of
> Judah and the streets of Jerusalem...
>
> *the voice of / / gladness / / and the voice of / / joy*
> *the voice of / / the groom / / and the voice of / / the bride.*
> (See Jeremiah 7:34, 16:9, 25:10, and 33:11)

Praised are you who causes the groom to rejoice with his bride. Through God, "the groom rejoices with his bride." This is the only allusion to the joys of sexual intimacy. It is otherwise not mentioned. But many see this last blessing as having a much deeper meaning. God himself is bound to Israel as by a bond of marriage. This marriage will be fully consummated only when Zion is restored. This is a wish that God will bring that day soon and that the young couple will be among those who live to see it. Thus this marriage (or new creation) prefigures the joy of the Messiah's coming (Trepp 287).

When the blessings were spoken, a cup of wine was passed to the couple in the same manner as before. This cup was called the "Cup of Sacrifice" and the "Cup of Salvation." They would have to share sacrifices in life, but eventually those sacrifices would be a source of salvation for both of them.

After drinking the wine, the groom broke the glass under foot amidst general rejoicing to cries of *Mazel tov!* (*Good Fortune!*) Sometimes a box filled with scent was broken and a pomegranate was crushed as a wish for the fertility of the couple.

The breaking of the glass reminded them that even at this time of supreme happiness, they must never allow themselves to forget the destruction of the temple and to always "rejoice with trembling," (Psalms 2:11) because the joys of earth are fleeting.

CHAPTER SEVEN

Gardens and Fountains

Now, only the consummation remained before the complete celebration would begin. The Bible is amazingly frank and unembarrassed in its references to sexual union as a basic human need and experience. Intense attraction was considered a blessing that brought about the purposes of God, and the coming together of the couple was a healthy fulfilling of the Creator's intention. Sexual intimacy was seen as an experience that allowed a man and a woman to act in a God-like role, in that through its expression, a husband and wife were empowered to create new life.

The world views sexuality as an uncontrollable desire. Religious hypocrisy views sexuality as dirty and degrading. Scriptures take the covenantal viewpoint that sexuality is a wholesome expression of physical intimacy as long as it is safeguarded under the commitment of marriage (Intrater 190).

In the Jewish New Testament, Hebrews 13:4 states:

Marriage is honorable in every respect; and in particular, sex within marriage is pure.

The feeling that marital relations are nasty or sordid is not scriptural. The Hebrew scriptures encourage a husband to "delight in [his] wife all [his] days" (Ecclesiastes 9:9) and to be "ravished (or infatuated) with love for her always" (Proverbs 5:19). In her devotional essay, Dorothy Patterson writes, "The Bible honors conjugal love and its romantic expression. One finds there a theology of sexuality which, as designed by God, offers unfailing beauty and incomparable worth.

Our Creator designed this most intimate union for His wise

purposes, some of which include:
- a.) to demonstrate the most absolute unity (Genesis 2:24);
- b.) to reveal knowledge on the ultimate level (Genesis 4:1);
- c.) to unleash the deepest comfort (Genesis 24:67; 2 Samuel 12:24);
- d.) to continue the generations through procreation (Genesis 1:28); [It's interesting to note that the capacity to procreate was a *blessing*—not only a commandment. "And God *blessed* them..."]
- e.) to guard against temptation (1 Corinthians 7:2-5). (Patterson 716)

A modern Jewish leader beautifully articulated the age-old teachings regarding the marriage relationship:

> Healthy intimacy requires two ingredients: discipline and sanctification. We must exercise self-control and we must also see sexuality as sacred. One must approach the sanctity of sexuality with awe, like entering into the Holy of Holies, where every action counts, where any blemish is intolerable. We must experience sexuality in a controlled environment with appropriate boundaries—not to dampen the expression of love, but to channel the powerful physical energies into healthy passion (Schneerson 70).

Marriage gave freedom of expression to pent-up desires, but also acted as a bridle to them. Marital satisfaction was considered a preventative to unfaithfulness and immorality. The marital "bridle" was designed to fill both partners with greater love for each other and increase their determination to remain faithful to their mutual covenant.

Faithfulness was imperative because covenant breaking was a betrayal of trust and an extremely grave sin (see Romans 1:31). After a marriage covenant was made, each partner assumed the commitment and responsibility to protect the intimacy that would be shared by the other person. Each intimate encounter was thought to represent a renewal of the marriage covenant. Sensitive intimacy is always vulnerable, and vulnerable intimacy is an important aspect of the holiness of marriage. To protect the vulnerability, an extremely high level of commitment was required (Intrater 13).

As a side note, the Biblical definition of "jealous" (or "zealous") includes having a fiery concern and determination to protect the intimacy of the covenant relationship. It is not about being possessive in a selfish way or showing immature insecurity. It is an appropriate reaction to the intense preciousness of the relationship with the other partner (Intrater 14-15).

Parents and religious leaders were given the charge to teach the young men and young women concerning the sanctity of sexuality and the laws that God wanted them to obey. Those laws allowed for a healthy intimacy that would enhance human growth. As with communicating all serious matters of truth, such teaching was to be done with love and discipline, in a manner and language that emphasized the positive. It was done privately in small groups, and of course, separately for boys and girls. Men taught the boys and women taught the girls.

It was felt that such instruction should be discreetly expressed. According to some rabbis, even the very language of scripture seemed to mandate modesty in discussing marital relations. "In the holy language," one observed, "no word at all has been laid down in order to designate either the male or the female organ of copulation, nor are there words designating the act itself that brings about generation....These are to be signified by terms used in a figurative sense and by allusions in the scriptures." (Maimonides - cited in *Women and Judaism* 3)

Scriptural euphemisms were employed for teaching purposes. "For the male organ, the Hebrew *gid* (sinew) and *shaphka* (instrument for pouring out)" were deemed acceptable (Lacks 3). "Feet," "thigh," "loins," and "flesh" were also used (Patai S&F 157). The terms for feminine capacity included "womb," "loins," "covering," and "flesh." The joint expression of intimacy was called "to know," "to rejoice with," "go in unto," "become one flesh," and "spend strength with." Great care was taken to avoid any provocative expressions or associations.

Parenthetically, in Genesis 24:2 and Genesis 47:29 we find the phrase "under my thigh." This symbolic gesture may have implied a curse of sterility upon the offender, if the covenant was broken. Sons were said to issue "from the thigh." This usage is found in the Hebrew text of Exodus 1:5 (Torah Commentary 161).

According to scholars, the Jewish faith had "an emphatically positive outlook on the value of legitimate sexual enjoyment" (Patai 164). The young people were schooled in their responsibilities and also their privileges concerning marital relations. The bridegroom was considered duty-bound to give his wife great joy and satisfaction in the act of intercourse. Mutual fulfillment and sexual equality were the goals and expectations. Rabbinic opinion in this matter agreed with Paul's teaching in 1 Corinthians 7:3-4:

> *Let the husband render unto the wife due benevolence: and likewise also the wife unto the husband. The wife hath not power of her own body, but the husband; and likewise also the husband hath not power of his own body, but the wife* (KJV).

A modern translation expresses the archaic terms in these verses more clearly:

> *The husband should not deprive his wife of sexual intimacy, which is her right as a married woman, nor should the wife deprive her husband. The wife gives authority over her body to her husband, and the husband also gives authority over his body to his wife* (NLT).

Of course, the spiritual nature of conjugal relations was also emphasized. Some of the principles and attitudes regarding feminine involvement are beautifully expressed in the following prayer offered before intercourse:

...purify my body, sanctify my soul and thoughts and intelligence and feelings. Strengthen me and dress me in Your good and generous spirit, that I might build up my household in truth and righteousness....Give this new life that may be conceived completeness in charity and mercy. Have compassion on all its doings, its health and creativity. Let nothing in its body be defective or wanting all the days of its life....Bless me and my household and my offspring with wholeness, completing our ideas and intelligence, and feeling, so that everything we do will be according to Thy will. Bless us with heavenly blessings from the world above. And from your blessings will Your servant's house be blessed all the days of our lives (Ragen 195).

A similar prayer familiar to men is found recorded in the apocryphal book of Tobit. It was offered by Tobias on his wedding night and is noteworthy for its disavowal of lust and the emphasis on enduring companionship (Collins 128).

"Blessed are you, O God of our ancestors...
You made Adam, and for him you made his wife Eve
   as a helper and support.
From the two of them the human race has sprung.
You said, "It is not good that the man should be alone;
   let us make a helper for him like himself."
I now am taking this kinswoman of mine,
   not because of lust, but with sincerity.
Grant that she and I may find mercy
   and that we may grow old together (Tobit 8:5-7)."

As implied in the wedding blessings and in this prayer, the model of being a "new Adam and Eve" was considered worthy of emulation. The wedding chamber would be a type of Eden–the beginning of a new creation–where they could begin the process of oneness in mind, heart, and body. It prefigured a congenial home that would be a scene of occupation and service for a happy and holy family. It also foreshadowed a millennial home of peace and perfection (Simpson 15).

After the bride and groom left the canopy, they were escorted to a beautifully prepared chamber. Today, this event is called *yichud* or seclusion. Modern Jewish couples spend approximately ten quiet minutes alone and undisturbed. If anyone asks where the couple is, they are told that they are "breaking their fast." Technically, this quiet time satisfies the legal requirement for opportunity to consummate the marriage. But anciently, only the process of "coming together" finished the "taking" required for legal recognition of the marriage.

The friend of the bridegroom completed one of his final duties by standing sentry outside of the chamber door while the couple consummated their marriage.

While we might feel a little self-conscious and awkward even discussing this event, the Jews acknowledged its accomplishment publicly in two ways. First of all, a garment or sheet from the marriage bed was carefully preserved by the girl's family as evidence that the two had become one. This was called the "token of virginity," because it had on it the small bloodstain that showed the bride's hymen had been broken and that she was a virgin until this first intimate encounter. This was immediately shown to witnesses at the wedding who would then be able to testify in her behalf, if needed, against future insinuations. Biblical law in this matter seems to indicate this was a prime source of legal protection for the wife (Deuteronomy 22:13-19).

The friend of the bridegroom, stationed at the threshold of the wedding chamber, had the task of listening carefully for the voice of the groom declaring that the nuptial rite had been successfully completed. When the announcement was heard, the friend was assured that he had fulfilled his year-long responsibility to watch over and deliver a chaste bride to her husband. In John 3:29, there is a reference concerning the friend's emotions at that time:

> "The friend of the bridegroom, who stands and hears him, *rejoices greatly* because of the bridegroom's voice."

The friend of the bridegroom jubilantly announced the marriage to guests who were waiting in a nearby room, and the week-long celebration began.

CHAPTER EIGHT

Food for Feasting

Major festive and social events in the Bible often centered around meals, and every meal was undergirded with spiritual understanding. Their purpose included much more than just the kindness of sharing food. The gestures of hospitality were considered by the Jews to be a sacred duty that reflected the righteous example of Father Abraham in Genesis 18:1-8:

> *One day about noon as Abraham was sitting at the entrance to his tent, he suddenly noticed three men standing nearby. He* got up, *and* ran to meet them, welcoming them *by* bowing low *to the ground. My lord,"* he said, *"if* it pleases you, stop here for a while. Rest *in the shade of this tree while* my servants get some water to wash your feet. Let me prepare some food *to refresh you.* Please stay *awhile before continuing on your journey."*
> *"All right,"* they said, *"Do as you have said."* So Abraham ran back *to the tent and said to Sarah, "Quick! Get three measures of your* best flour *and* bake some bread." *Then Abraham ran out to* the herd to choose a fat calf *and told a servant to* hurry *and* prepare it. *When the food was ready, he took some cheese curds, and milk, and the roasted meat, and he served it to the men. As they ate, Abraham waited on* them *beneath the trees* (NLT).

The emphasized words serve to convey the gracious sense of urgency that kept Abraham occupied while showing lavish hospitality. This incident is alluded to in Hebrews 13:2,

> Be not *forgetful to entertain strangers, for thereby* some have entertained angels unawares (KJV).

The word "entertain" can also be translated as "show love to" (RSV), "show hospitality to" (TEV), "be friendly to" (JNT), and "welcome" (NJB). These actions were a moral obligation for every family in Israel. According to one Middle Eastern scholar,

> The hospitality of the Eastern peoples exceeds all their other virtues. While the greetings of peace from a visitor are received by the host of the house, the women immediately rush to take the shoes from his feet...and bring cold water to wash them. (After being offered a drink) and as a mark of genuine hospitality, a guest is asked as often as seven times to eat. The guest refuses by saying, "Thank you. I have just eaten. I am not hungry." But the host insists by holding on to his garment and urging him, saying, "By God and his Holy Scriptures, you must eat." This is the custom to which Jesus referred in the parable about compelling guests to attend *(My Neighbor Jesus* 45).

There were times when a guest was not welcome and none of the members of the house would rise to meet him. George Lamsa tells of such an experience and the response of the rejected guest:

> The guest's greetings of peace are returned to him in such a cold manner that he immediately understands that he is not welcome. At such discourtesy, the visitor then loosens the straps of his sandals and shakes the sand out. When this is done near the entrance of the house, it signified that the house has broken the sacred code of hospitality. The dust became a witness. The tired and dusty traveler will refuse to even quench his thirst in that house (MNJ 46).

But such occasions were quite rare. Because of Abraham's experience, they believed that every stranger potentially carried a divine message. To reject the stranger would also be a rejection of the Lord whose message he bore. The host would, by such an action, offend God and cut himself off from further opportunities to receive such important communications. Generally, Middle

Easterners were more willing to feed and shelter even their enemies rather than gain a reputation for being inhospitable.

Banquets and feasts have been used by every culture to celebrate important events and provide entertainment. But at the time of Christ, there was a marked contrast between the revelry of the neighboring Greco-Roman culture and the Jews who saw banquets and feasts as having ritual and spiritual significance. The table in every home was thought to be a type of the temple altar and foods placed upon them were thought to symbolize the covenant offerings given there.

"*Hag*" is one of the Hebrew words for "feast", and is commonly associated with wedding feasts. "*Hag*" or "*chag*" is derived from the root word *"chagag"* (Strong 2287), which means "to move in a circle, to march in a sacred procession, to celebrate, to dance, to hold a solemn feast." (Haggai means "born on a feast day.") Many spiritual traditions relating to celebratory meals reflected temple associations and the covenant offerings given there, especially on religious feast days. According to Juengst,

> ...hospitality was marked by another element that lifted it above the realm of simple human kindness and generosity. The guest meal was not only festal, but had a sacrificial nature as well. Killing an animal was regarded as a sacrificial act. Therefore, when meat was eaten on festal occasions, it carried sacred significance. Even the bread cakes, the second most important ingredient of the guest meal, were associated with sacrificial feasts (see 2 Samuel 6:19 and Juengst 41).

The fatted calf was the meat that carried the most status at meals, followed by lamb and then a young goat or kid. This is reflected in the parable of the Prodigal Son where the older son attempted to emphasize how unfairly he had been treated by his father,

> *And he answering said to his father, Lo, these many years do I serve thee...yet thou never gavest me a kid, that I might make merry with my friends: But as soon as this thy son was come...thou hast killed for him the fatted calf* (Luke 15: 29-30).

Meat was not the only food associated with sacred offerings and feasts. Other foods also had this significance. Among these were the "seven species" listed in Deuteronomy 8:8. These were the seven kinds of produce that were considered acceptable to bring as "first fruit offerings" or *"bikkurim"* to the temple. These foods and their by-products symbolized many of God's greatest blessings to man. They were held in high esteem and always served at wedding feasts along with other symbolic foods.

The "seven species" or foods were wheat, barley, grapes, figs, pomegranates, olives, and dates ("honey"). Their individual significance will be discussed separately.

THE SEVEN SPECIES

Wheat & Barley

The first two products are generally listed as "corn" in the King James Version of the scriptures. Even today in the Middle East, wheat fields are known as "corn fields." (Moldenke 232). However, the yellow cobs that we are familiar with did not exist in Bible times. Read "grain" wherever "corn" appears in the Bible.

The very finest wheat was tithed at the temple—it was known as "the fat kidneys of wheat" (see Deuteronomy 32:14). The Hebrews used "fat" as an idiom to describe the best of a thing. In modern English, an equivalent expression would be "the cream of the crop."

Wheat and barley were primarily ground into flour for bread, but they were also eaten boiled and parched, soaked and roasted, or even green from the stalk. Because wheat and other grains were such an important part of everyday survival, they became an important religious symbol. An abundant harvest was a blessing from God, and famines were taken as a sign of His displeasure.

Bread has fascinating associations for Eastern people. It was believed to provide spiritual as well as physical sustenance. All bread brought to mind the time when the Israelites found themselves without food after leaving Egypt. It was then that a loving heavenly Father rained down "bread from heaven" or "manna" to sustain them. According to legend, manna had miraculous properties: to children, it tasted like mother's milk; to youths, like bread; to the old, like honey; and to the sick like barley soaked in oil and honey (Exodus Rabbah 25:3).

A meal was defined, in the Jewish view, by the inclusion of bread on the table. Since bread was the staple food of man, its presence or absence determined whether a meal had been eaten and if blessings needed to be offered. If one ate a piece of bread at least the size of an olive, then it was counted as a meal. On the other hand, even if a large quantity of cake was consumed, it was not considered a meal.

To "break bread" meant "to eat a meal." Bread was always broken or torn; it was never cut. Since it was considered a gift from God, only fingers were thought appropriate to touch it. Normally, a Middle Easterner would not tell a lie if there was bread on the table. Bread was thought to represent God's presence at the table, and it was unthinkable to be dishonest in His presence (Errico 75).

One Middle Eastern author, Dr. Abraham Rihbany, shared his understanding about bread,

> I was brought up to think of bread as possessing a mystic sacred significance. I would never step on a piece of bread fallen in the road, but would pick it up, press it to my lips for reverence, and place it in a wall or some other place where it would not be trodden upon. What always seemed to me to be one of the noblest traditions of my people was their reverence for bread–literally "the life-giver" (Rihbany 95).

At the beginning of a meal, a blessing over bread was recited,

> "Blessed are you, O Lord our God, King of the Universe, who brings forth bread from the earth."

After the blessing, a small piece of bread was salted and eaten. This emphasized the similarity between the table and the altar in the temple, and between the food and sacrifices. All sacrifices in the temple were required to be salted (Leviticus 2:13). It was believed that bread and salt went together because the letter comprising the word *melah*—salt—are identical with the letters of *lehem*—bread. Salt had an additional association with the sin-offerings offered on the altar of the temple. The Hebrew word *mahal*—"to forgive"—has the same root word as *melah*, salt.

As a side note, after a meal was completed, *Birkat ha-Mazon* or "Grace after Meals" was recited. This practice was based on the principle of Deuteronomy 8:10:

> *When thou hast eaten and are full, then thou shalt bless the Lord thy God.*

Immediately before *birkat ha-mazon*, it was customary for all knives to be removed from the table. Since the table represented the altar, the injunction given in Exodus 20:25 was applied:

> *You shall not build it (the altar) of hewn stones, for if you lift up your sword on it, you will have profaned it.*
> (Hebrew Trans.)

By a sword, an instrument made of iron (or steel) was meant, and a knife fell into that category. Furthermore, the Bible describes the work involved in building the temple of Solomon,

> *Neither hammer nor axe, nor any tool of iron was heard in the house while it was being built* (I Kings 6:7 [Hebrew Trans.]).

So while God was being praised for the festive and bountiful table (symbolic of the altar which promoted spiritual peace and emotional contentment) the knife, as a prototype of the sword which brought death and destruction and sadness could not be present (Minhagim 89).

Grapes (The Vine)

The Hebrew word rendered "vine" is still in use today for "grapes." The grape-vine was used as a symbol for the Jewish people ("the fruitful vine" and the "vine brought out of Egypt") and Jesus compared himself to that "true vine" of which his disciples were the branches. The grape-vine was the very first plant to be recorded in the Bible as cultivated (Genesis 9:20). Rebellious Israelites were compared to "wild grapes," "an empty vine," and "the degenerate plant of a strange vine." The phrases "sour grapes" and "grapes of wrath" represent the harvest—or consequences—of a person's deeds.

The grape-vine was a conventional fertility symbol. The image of a vine was a popular one on *ketubot* (marriage contracts) along with the Biblical verse: "Your wife shall be as a fruitful vine in the innermost parts of your house" (Psalms 128:3).

Grapes were also a harvest symbol. Since the grape harvest occurred in the Fall when most weddings took place, it was seen as enhancing a time of great joy and celebration.

As a food, grapes were eaten fresh, dried as raisins, or boiled down to a syrup known as grape "honey." As a drink, grapes could be processed to make juice, vinegar, or wine.

There are three categories of references to wine or drinking in scripture.
- where wine is mentioned, but neither endorsed nor condemned
- where wine is identified as a source of misery
- where wine is identified as a blessing in conjunction with bread and oil

In *Bible Wines, or Laws of Fermentation and Wines of the Ancients*, William Patton writes:

> There were...two kinds of wine in ancient use. The one was sweet, pleasant, refreshing, unfermented; the other was exciting, inflaming, and intoxicating. Each was called wine (132).

Patton meticulously documents the fact that unfermented beverages, called wines, existed and were used by the ancients. He gives abundant proof of the generic nature of the two Hebrew words *Yayin* and *Shakar*.

- *Yayin* (translates as "wine") designates grape juice, or the liquid which the fruit of the vine yields. This may be new or old, sweet or sour, fermented or unfermented, intoxicating or non-intoxicating. (56)

- *Shakar* (translates as "strong drink") "signifies 'sweet drink' expressed from fruits other than the grape, and drunk in an unfermented or fermented state." (57-58)

In ancient Israel, wine was valued because it provided an important dietary liquid in a hot region characterized by scarce and frequently contaminated water. But too much of the intoxicating variety was considered unhealthy and imprudent. Priests were forbidden to drink wine while performing their sacred duties (Leviticus 10:9). One of those sacred duties was to pour the wine and water libation as an offering on the altar in the temple (Richman 43).

Olives

The olive was definitely one of the most valuable and versatile trees in the Holy Land, and was referenced in many passages about olives, olive trees, olive groves, and olive oil. One botanist who has made a long and careful study of the healing plants of the Bible says that,

> No tree is more closely associated with the history of man and the development of civilization than the olive (Moldenke 158).

Biblical gardens (such as the Garden of Gethsemane) were usually olive orchards where one could

> Biblical gardens (such as the Garden of Gethsemane) were usually olive orchards where one could retire during the heat of the day and find relief from the scorching sun. The olive was valued as a source of fruit, oil, and wood. To the people of the Middle East, it was a symbol of peace, prosperity and divine blessing, beauty, luxuriance, and strength (Moldenke 159).

Along with bread and wine, olive oil was tithed at the temple and eaten there in a sacral meal "before the Lord."

> And thou shalt eat before the Lord thy God, in the place which he shall choose to place his name (the Temple), the tithe of thy bread, of thy wine, and of thine oil..(Deuteronomy 14:23).

This food trio is also mentioned in Psalms 104:15 where the Lord blesses man so that he can produce "*wine* to make him happy (cheer his heart), *oil* to make him cheerful (make his face shine), and *bread* to give him strength (sustain his life).

The olive has long been a symbol of divine blessing. The shine produced by anointing one's skin with it was thought to be a type of the shining radiance of the Divine Presence. In Numbers 6:25, the Lord told Moses to bless the children of Israel and say,

> *The Lord make* his face to shine *upon thee and be gracious [deal kindly] unto thee.*

Olive oil is a high energy food and one of the most digestible of all fats. The people of Biblical days found ways to incorporate it somehow in nearly every meal, both for cooking and for table use.

Olive oil was also used as a fuel, as part of religious ceremonial anointings, as a cosmetic, and to offer guests as a sign of welcome. Olive oil was mixed with wine and used to soften and soothe wounds–as in the parable of the Good Samaritan.

Because of its potential to live over 2,000 years and still bear fruit, the olive tree has long represented longevity and immortality. It takes eight years before a tree generally begins producing fruit; and it propagates by putting out shoots, insuring its continued survival even as its main trunk becomes hollow. In Psalms 128:3, children are compared to "olive shoots around your table", the image is that of branches springing up from the roots around a trunk that has been cut off. The olive is also an evergreen and can flourish in extremely rocky areas (Frankel 123).

Figs

Figs are one of the "seven species" (Deuteronomy 8:8) that are specified to symbolize the fertility of the promised land. Beginning with the Garden of Eden, the fig is mentioned more than fifty-five times in the Bible. In Genesis 3:7, it is the first fruit specifically named.

In ancient Israel, virtually every private garden had a fig tree in one corner, both for the shade, and for the sweet delicious fruit which was very nourishing. At the time of Christ, figs were especially popular with athletes who ate them specifically to increase their stamina and improve their performance (Ward 26).

In Biblical terms, the fig represented peace, prosperity, and great joy. In connection with the vine, it was used to represent a type of millennial existence where families could multiply and flourish in safety. In Micah 4:4, we read of this:

> *But they shall sit every man under his vine and under his fig tree: and none shall make them afraid...*

The fig was often used to typify the people of Israel. The prophets Hosea and Jeremiah made use of them for analogies:

> *I found Israel like grapes in the wilderness; I saw your fathers as the first ripe in the fig tree at her first time...*(Hosea 9:10).

and

> ...behold, two baskets of figs were set before the temple of the Lord...One basket had very good figs, even like the figs that are first ripe: and the other basket had very naughty (worthless) figs which could not be eaten, they were so bad. Then said the Lord unto me, What seest thou, Jeremiah? And I said Figs; the good figs very good and the evil, very evil, that cannot be eaten they are so evil.... Thus saith the Lord; Like these good figs, so will I acknowledge them that are carried away of Judah.... For I will set mine eyes upon them for good....And as the evil figs,...I will deliver them...to be removed...for their hurt...to be a reproach...and a curse...whither I shall drive them (Jeremiah 24:1-9).

The tree that brought forth "hasty fruit" (Isaiah 28:4), "good fruit" (Matthew 7:17-20), and "summer fruit" (Amos 8:1-2) was also the fig. "Bethphage" means "house of figs" and was the location where Christ cursed the barren fig tree so that it withered completely away (Matthew 21:1,19-21). Fig leaves were used as a sign for the events of the last days (Matthew 24:32). And they were also used metaphorically in Joel to describe the destruction of Israel.

> They hath laid my vine waste, and splintered my fig trees. They have stripped off the bark and thrown it away. The vine has dried up and the fig tree withered (Tanakh - Joel 1:7, 12).

As an aside, in Biblical thought, the idiom to be "dried up" meant that a woman could no longer bear children. To be "withered" sometimes meant that a man could no longer father children.

A good friend, Joy Perry, in our personal correspondence, pointed out some fascinating facts concerning figs and their associations with the blessings of fertility. She found her references in *Webster's Dictionary*, a medical book, and botanical encyclopedia. Reproduced below are some illustrations and comments from those sources.

Fig Plant   Fig (Cross section)

Because Joy's background is in the medical field, she could not help noticing some similarities between the fig in its stages of development and the development of the human embryo. The comparisons are shown below.

Fig Pulp - "False Fruit"
Fig Seed - "True Fruit"

Fruit of the Womb

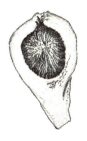 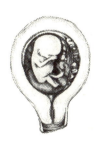

Fig Female Flower   Human Fallopian Tubes

Heavenly Father's illustrations for teaching us are truly remarkable. It is beyond the scope of this book, but an interested reader will find much food for thought in studying more about this fruit and its cultivation.

Pomegranates

The Hebrew word translated "pomegranate" is "*rimmon*" or "bell." Pomegranates are notable for their beautiful red flowers, shapely fruit, sweet flavor (to those in the Middle East!), and prodigious number of seeds. The fruit is the size of an orange and has a calyx which resembles a crown.

Because of its decorative form, it has long been a poplar motif in Jewish art. The flowers of the pomegranate served as patterns for the "golden bells" and also for "open flowers" embroidered on the temple robes of the High Priest. Fabric pomegranates adorned the hem of the robe, alternating with golden bells. The erect calyx-lobes on the fruit served as inspiration for Solomon's crown, and incidentally, for all crowns from that time on.

Israelites were exhorted by their sages to "be as full of good deeds as a pomegranate is full of seeds," and good students were said to model their study habits upon the pomegranate, eating only the good fruit, but discarding the bitter peel (Hagigah 15b).

The pulp of the fruit has long been used to make cooling drinks and sherbets and is also eaten raw. A popular spiced wine is also made from pomegranates. Their soft red seeds are eaten raw, sprinkled with sugar, and are also dried as a sort of candy.

The astringent rind of the unripened fruit has been used for medicine; and the Moors introduced a method of tanning leather with pomegranate rinds that made Cordoba famous for its fine leather.

In some parts of the Middle East today, a bride casts a ripe pomegranate to the ground and the number of seeds that drop out indicates the number of children she will have (Moldenke 191).

Dates ("Honey")

The word "honey" (Hebrew: *d'vash*) was not always used in

the sense that we use it today. Bees are mentioned in the Bible only four times, while "honey" is mentioned forty-nine times (Moldenke 171).

According to the Jewish leaders, the "honey" of the "seven species" is not bee honey, but date honey—the syrup squeezed from ripe dates (Jerusalem Talmud, Bikkurim 1,3). [For a more complete discussion of this subject, see *Nature in Our Biblical Heritage* by Nogah Hareuveni.]

In ancient times, date palms covered large areas of Jerusalem. Palms require a good deal of careful cultivation. They must grow thirty years to reach full maturity and they then continued bearing for another seventy years. Because the palm is dioecious (meaning that palm trees are either male or female), they must be in close proximity for fertilization to occur. In warfare, the greatest calamity that could be inflicted upon the conquered was the destruction of their male date palms.

The palm was symbolic of Israel, and to commemorate the subjection of the Jews and the destruction of Israel in 70 AD, the Roman emperor, Vespasian, issued a coin, showing a weeping woman sitting beneath a palm tree.

Coin

The date palm (Hebrew: *Tamar*) has a tall, shapely form and palms were frequently used in temple designs. In Biblical poetry, palms symbolized beauty, grace, and fruitfulness. Their immense leaves ("branches" in the Bible) were symbols of triumph and were used on occasions of great rejoicing. For example, in Revelations 7:9 we read:

> *After this I beheld a great multitude...which no man could number...who stood before the throne and before the lamb, clothed with white robes, and palms in their hands....*(KJV).

John 12:12-13 recounts another event where palms were used to show great respect:

> *The next day the great crowd...heard that Jesus was on his way to Jerusalem. They took palm branches and went out to meet him shouting..."Blessed is He who comes in the name of the Lord!"* (NIV)

The name He-Who-Comes was one of the names for the Messiah and is found in Psalms 118:26 (Sabourin 315).

The Arabs have a saying that there are as many uses for the palm as there are days in the year. Its large leaves are used to cover roofs and the sides of houses. Mats, baskets, and dishes are constructed with them. Small leaves are used as dusters, and the wood of its trunk for timber. Rope is made from the web-like material at the top and its fruit is a chief article of food.

The kernel of the date is ground up or soaked in water for several days and used as food for cows, camels, and sheep. It is said to be more nutritious than barley.

Date seeds are also strung as beads, and fermented date juice is often the intoxicating liquor referred to as "strong drink" in the Bible. Along with raisins, the dates were thought to be especially invigorating for men fighting in battle. In the Greco-Roman culture at the time of Christ, the date palm symbolized worldly riches, procreation, victory, and light.

ADDITIONAL FOODS FOR FEASTING

Bread

Bread and cakes were a mainstay in the Israelite diet, and these were served at wedding feasts without exception. On such occasions, generous abundance and variety were the rule.

Neighbors would often contribute gifts of food, brought on trays, and bread and cakes were especially appreciated. A description of some festive kinds is given by Mackie:

> There are crisp network discs covered with sesame seeds, paste buns filled with ground nuts and folded in a triangular shape; threads of (dough) are twisted together to the thickness of a rope, steeped in a sauce of honey and nuts, and arranged in a flat coil to make a large cake served on a flat tray; thin wafers are coated with grape "honey" and powdered with pungent, fragrant seeds, and also cakes fried in oil (105).

It was customary to place three small "loaves" of bread at each setting. These resembled modern tortillas or pancakes. Pieces of this bread were doubled up, spoon fashion, and used to scoop up the stews and sauces. By practice, this was done with much expert cleanliness and was not at all messy. When one prepared such a mouthful and handed it to another at the table, it was a sign of friendly regard. An affectionate exchange of food would take place only between friends. In some parts of the Middle East, this "sop" is called "the bread of friendship." In John 13:26, we read of such an exchange:

> *Jesus answered, He it is, to whom I shall give a sop, when I have dipped it. And when he had dipped the sop, he gave it to Judas Iscariot...*

Through the sharing of his sop, Jesus truly practiced his own teaching—to "love your enemies."

Meat

The addition of meat to a menu defined a meal as a feast. The most common popular dish was lamb, which was roasted whole and stuffed with seasoned rice and vegetables. This was generally served on a large copper tray. The meat was so thoroughly cooked and tender that it separated easily from the bone. It was lifted off and eaten with the fingers of the right hand in such portions as one desired.

It was common for the host of a banquet to show favor and honor by selecting choice morsels from a common dish and personally feeding them to the chosen guest. This practice still exists in some areas, and the recipients occasionally discover that it can be a "somewhat depressing honor." Barbara Bowen writes of such an experience:

> If you are a guest in their home, the polite "Oriental" will tear up the best bits and put them in your mouth. I have had this done for me.... Once my hostess placed some bits of meat in her own mouth and evidently found the taste extra fine, so she immediately removed the choice morsel and placed it in my mouth....Well, you must look pleased and honored (84).

In Bible times, one extra-special and coveted dish was the "fat-tail" of a particular kind of sheep. These sheep were bred especially for their tails which weighed up to thirty pounds. The tails were so heavy that a special cart was constructed to support and protect them. In the tractate *Shabbat*, it was forbidden to "let out the sheep with their little carts" on the Sabbath (Mishnah Shabbat 5:4).

This tail is mentioned in Exodus 29:22, Leviticus 3:9, and 9:19. It was specified as a sacrificial offering in the temple. Possibly Isaiah had this tail cart in mind as a visual aid when he wrote Isaiah 5:18...

> *Woe unto those who draw iniquity with cords of vanity and sin as it were with a cart rope.*

Although certain portions of fat were prohibited (particularly the fat surrounding vital organs) under the Mosaic law (Leviticus 3:17), the fat-tail was highly desirable as food. Its flavor has been described as delicious, not too rich, and

Sheep with tail cart

tasting rather like marrow bones.

All meats were served with spicy sauces. These were flavored with mustard, cumin, dill, coriander, or mint, as well as garlic and onions.

Although the rabbis were not in agreement about the camel, and sometimes forbade the use of its milk, the Bedouins devised the world's largest (according to Guinness) wedding dish from it.

> The largest item on any menu in the world is roasted camel, prepared occasionally for Bedouin wedding feasts. Cooked eggs are stuffed into fish, the fish stuffed into a cooked chickens, the chickens stuffed into a roasted sheep's carcass and the sheep stuffed into a whole camel (18).

Vegetables and Fruits

In Bible times there were no tomatoes, corn, bananas, pears, or strawberries. The most common vegetables were beans, lentils, cucumbers, lettuce and leeks. Melons, oranges, figs, raisins, and apricots served as dessert for the meal. Chocolate was unknown. Walnuts were popular and were thought to bring good luck and good health. Pistachios and almonds were treats; and the latter was thought to have a religious significance. Jewish tradition said that the staff of the coming Messiah would be an almond branch.

Beverages

Red wine, often mixed with honey, was the drink of choice on these festive occasions. Middle Eastern people also drank a great deal of water. While sitting at the table, a small hand pitcher (*cruse*) was continually passed around. Everyone drank from the same container, and they were able to drink from the spout of the jar without touching it to their lips. They could easily detect the subtle taste differences of water. In a town with several public fountains, the guests could decisively tell from which well the water in the pitcher had been taken. The longing expressed by David in 2 Samuel 23:15 for a drink from a specific well in Bethlehem was well understood, and everyone could have empathized with his yearning.

Two scriptures reflect the custom set for the length of the feast.

> *Finish this daughter's bridal week; and then we will give you the younger one also, in return for another seven years of work* (Genesis 29:27 NIV).

and

> *Let me tell you a riddle,"* Samson said to them. *"If you can give me the answer within the seven days of the feast, I will give you thirty linen garments and thirty sets of clothes"* (Judges 14:12 NIV).

In Hebrew, "seven" is *"shevah."* It is from the root *"savah,"* which means "to be full," "to be satisfied," or "to have enough of" (Bullinger 167). It is a number that is associated with weddings through seven species, seven feast days, seven nuptial blessings, and through Jehovah's seven-fold covenant promises with Israel at Sinai.

The verbs "bring," "take," and "redeem" have special wedding associations to the Jews.

The promises are found in Exodus 6:6-8:

- I will *bring* you out from Egypt
- I will rid you of their bondage
- I will *redeem* you
- I will *take* you to Me for a people
- I will be to you a God
- I will *bring* you into the land
- I will give it (to) you for an heritage

The wedding week was similar to a modern open house with out-of-town guests staying at the home of the groom's father. Not everyone stayed for the entire week, or returned for lengthy (five to six hours) celebrating every late afternoon, for the demands of life were heavy on ordinary folks in Israel. But each evening of the bridal week brought some renewal of the festivities, and all who had been invited were warmly received until the week was over and everyone went back to their usual routine.

As each guest arrived, the servants would provide water for washing hands from stone jars kept specifically for this purpose. Jars of stone were not subject to ritual defilement as was earthenware; and ritual purity was important for guests who strictly observed the rabbinic custom of multiple washings.

Additionally, when a feast was given, a servant frequently stood by the door with perfumed water, such as rose water or orange blossom water. The guests were sprinkled when they entered the home. The sprinkling was understood to fit them for the presence of their host, to declare them his guests, and as such, to place them under his favor and protection. Perfuming fitted one for the marriage feast (Bowen 85).

Scholarly opinion varies, but according to some authorities, the wedding week began with an intimate "marriage supper," not to be confused with the later wedding feast. This was eaten in the wedding chamber by the bride and groom plus a few chosen friends known as "the children of the bridechamber" (*b'nai huppah*). These selected friends would be witnesses to the promises made by the groom to his new bride concerning their happy future, which promises would be ratified with a pinch of salt.

While the new couple "honeymooned" in their chamber, much merriment and festivities were enjoyed by the wedding guests. During the seven-day period, whenever the couple made their appearance, the guests would clap and cheer and congratulate them. In keeping with tradition, the couple were treated and addressed as though they were a king and queen and were seated on special chairs intended to represent thrones.

It was considered a religious duty to have music, and flutes were traditionally played before the bridal pair. It is interesting to note that flutes were used in the Jewish temple liturgy as a type of the Messiah—"the pierced one"—and the hope for his return to redeem Israel was echoed in many wedding songs.

Raphael Patai has translated one of these songs. It is found on page 234 in his book *Jewish Folklore*.

1. You became a bridegroom, be blessed,
   God behind you be your shield,
   Long life be with you,
   With a good name in Israel.
   Send the Redeemer, send the Redeemer!

2. Your stature like a free cedar,
   Your face like the moon which God gave,
   Like Joseph, a cypress branch,
   Be a hero in Israel.
   Send the Redeemer, send the Redeemer!

3. God be your guardian,
   Let Him give success in all your deeds,
   Wise like Jacob the prophet,
   With heart's desire in Israel.
   Send the Redeemer, send the Redeemer!

4. All my friends and well-wishers,
   The banquet guests and the princes,
   Sing a hundred thousand songs,
   The community of the people of Israel.
   Send the Redeemer, send the Redeemer!

5. In a good sign you become a bridegroom,
   May God be your shield,
   Be victorious over Satan,
   Strong in the religion of Israel.
   Send the Redeemer, send the Redeemer!

6. Rejoice in your spouse,
   The noble one, whom God gave
   To be your spouse: she was sent
   By the God of Israel.
   Send the Redeemer, send the Redeemer!

7. In those seven days you are free,
   Them you shall spend in joy,
   But let yourself not fall away
   From the law of the religion of Israel
   Send the Redeemer, send the Redeemer!

8. O bridegroom, be capable,
   May what you hope come to you,
   In your days let there be and received
   A gate of plenty in Israel.
   Send the Redeemer, send the Redeemer!

9. May your bride give you satisfaction.
   Let your heart be free of sorrow,
   She will build your house,
   With a good name in Israel.
   Send the Redeemer, send the Redeemer!

10. We shall come with a willing heart,
    With two eyes we shall see,
    Bring the Shekhina for us,
    All the people of Israel.
    Send the Redeemer, send the Redeemer!

Many scholars believe that a collection of "mini-songs," today known as *The Song of Solomon*, was also sung at weddings. Anyone under thirty was forbidden to listen to or to read the lyrics. John J. Collins relates more concerning this matter:

> The fact that *The Song of Solomon* was accepted as scripture was probably dependent on an allegorical interpretation, which took the lovers as God and Israel. We learn from the Talmud, however, that some people sang it in banquet halls as a secular air, although the rabbis deemed that such people brought evil on the world. (b. Sanhedrin 101 a.) (136-137)

The guests also danced, acted out plays and made up poems and riddles. Each guest desired to increase the joy and happiness of the newly married couple. All were to rejoice together. A rabbinic ruling said that the marriage guests were relieved of all religious observances that would lessen their joy. This was interpreted to mean that everyone was exempt from fasting during this period. The remarks of Jesus in Mark 2:19-20 reflect this understanding.

> *And Jesus said unto them, Can the children of the bridechamber fast, while the bridegroom is with them? As long as they have the bridegroom with them, they cannot fast. But the days will come, when the bridegroom shall be taken away from them, and then shall they fast in those days.*

A time of great grief and distress in Israel is poignantly portrayed in Psalms 78:63 by the loss of this happy time:

> *Fire consumed their young men, and their maidens had no wedding songs* (NIV).

Seating

Middle Eastern etiquette demanded that the seating at banquets follow rigid protocol. Considerable attention was given to the status, seniority, family dignity, and official positions of the various guests, and they were arranged according to their age and social standing. The most important guests sat nearest the bride and groom and furthest from the door. This location was elevated and had thick comfortable cushions. The best food in the most plentiful amounts was also located in this area.

It was considered good form for guests to make several protests of self-abasement—each esteeming the other better than himself—before being seated. Among the Jews, a man instructed in the Law of Torah, although poor in worldly goods, was considered superior to a rich man who had little religious position. It was the reverence of heart towards God's service which the Pharisees accepted and abused when they claimed for themselves the place of honor at social and religious assemblies (Mackie 105).

The least important guests were the beggars, musicians, and the young people. They sat near the door on mats or low seats with small pillows. The servants also stood in this area.

Latecomers frequently took a seat near the door so as not to be disruptive, but the host did not hesitate to regulate the position of his guests if the latecomer was of noble position. He would first send a servant to notify one of the other guests that he had to go down to a lower seat. The servant would say, "Get up and go down, an honorable guest is coming." Then the host would promptly usher the more distinguished guest to a higher place as a token of honor.

It was to avoid this unseemly embarrassment and confusion that Jesus in Luke 14:7-11 instructed his disciples to take the lower seats at banquets.

> *When he noticed how the guests picked the places of honor at the table, he told them this parable: When someone invites you to a wedding feast, do not take the place of honor, for a person more distinguished than you may have been invited. If so, the host who invited both of you will come and say to you, "Give this man your seat."*
>
> *Then, humiliated, you will have to take the least important place. But when you are invited, take the lowest place, so that when your host comes, he will say to you, "Friend, move up to a better place." Then you will be honored in the presence of all your fellow guests. For everyone who exalts himself will be humbled, and he who humbles himself will be exalted* (NIV).

Party Manners

Besides the careful attention paid to seating arrangements, there were other polite behaviors to be observed. We can find, in the apocryphal book of Ecclesiasticus, a passage on party manners that is very instructive:

> If you are sitting down to a lavish table, do not display your greed or say, "What a lot to eat!"... Do not reach out for anything your host has his eye on, do not jostle him at the dish....Be thoughtful, eat what is offered you, and do not wolf down your food or you will earn dislike. For politeness' sake, be the first to stop; do not act the glutton or you will give offense. If you are forced to eat too much, get up, go and vomit, and you will feel better (Ecclus 31:12-21 NJB).

It was customary for the older men to give wise counsel at the table as part of the entertainment. Their opinions were highly respected, but some of them occasionally didn't understand that it was possible to have too much of a good thing. There was a scriptural exhortation for them also:

> Speak, old man—it is proper that you should—but with discretion: do not spoil the music. If someone is singing, do not ramble on and do not play the sage at the wrong moment (Ecclus 32:3-4).

Wise counsel concerning appropriate behavior for the younger men was also given, so that they might not embarrass themselves.

> Speak young man, when you must but twice at most, and then only if questioned. Keep to the point, say much in few words; give the impression of knowing but not wanting to speak. Among eminent people do not behave as though you were their equal; do not make frivolous remarks when someone else is speaking (Ecclus. 32: 7-9).

The cautions about wine prevented contention when they were followed.

> When there are many about you, do not be quick to stretch out your hand, or quick to call for wine. Do not play the [glutton] at your wine, for wine has been the undoing of many. Drunk at the right time and in the right amount, wine makes for a glad heart and a cheerful mind. Bitterness of soul comes of wine drunk to excess out of temper or bravado. Do not provoke your fellow-guest at a wine feast, do not make fun of him when he is enjoying himself, do not take him to task or annoy him by reclaiming money owed (Ecclus. 31:25-31).

Generally, one of the groom's friends was appointed as the "ruler," "governor," or "presider," at the wedding feast. This was a position of honor and trust; and it was his job to see that the food and drink were readily supplied, and that the wedding festivities ran smoothly. The author of Ecclesiasticus, Ben Sirach, had suggestions for him also:

> Have they made you the presider? Do not let it go to your head, behave like everyone else in the party, see that they are happy and then sit down yourself. Having discharged your duties, take your place so that your joy may be through theirs, and you may receive the crown for your competence (Ecclus. 32:1-2 NJB).

> Spread the table, and the quarrel will end.
> Hebrew Proverb

This proverb expresses one of the many social benefits of feasting. It was a time when relationships were reaffirmed, repaired, and strengthened by eating together. The ancient Biblical understanding also encompassed the idea that, when the Messiah came, He would entertain His people at a great Messianic Banquet. Isaiah spoke of God preparing for His people "a feast of fat things, a feast of wine on the lees, of fat things

This proverb expresses one of the many social benefits of feasting. It was a time when relationships were reaffirmed, repaired, and strengthened by eating together. The ancient Biblical understanding also encompassed the idea that, when the Messiah came, He would entertain His people at a great Messianic Banquet. Isaiah spoke of God preparing for His people "a feast of fat things, a feast of wine on the lees, of fat things full of marrow, of wine on the lees well refined" (Isaiah 25:6). Jesus spoke of many coming from the east and the west and sitting down with the Patriarchs in the kingdom of heaven (Matthew 8:11). The word used for "sitting down" is the word for "reclining at a meal." The picture is of all men sitting down together—forgiven, bonded to each other, rejoicing, and feasting in the fullest sense. Jesus at the Last Supper said that he would not again drink of the cup until he drank it new in his Father's kingdom. This foreshadowed the great Messianic banquet or Marriage Feast of the Lamb spoken of in Revelations (Barclay 175).

When we grasp the spiritual meaning of food, we understand that "feasts are to be joyous playful reminders of who we are, opportunities for expressing gratitude for God's abundant love, and symbolic reenactments of the harmonious gathering to come at the Lord's kingdom table (Juengst 87)."

CHAPTER NINE

Song for the Bridegroom

On the first Sabbath morning following the marriage, the groom entered the synagogue, escorted by his male companions. There he was conducted by the elders to a seat of honor, next to the *Aron-ha-Kodesh* or Ark of the Law, where the Torah scrolls were kept. This was the first occasion on which he was permitted to put on the *tallit* (prayer shawl) which his bride had given him after their betrothal, for it could only be worn by a married man. Wrapped in its flowing folds, the groom ascended the three steps to the platform (*bema*) to read aloud from the weekly portion of the Torah. Thereupon, the entire congregation burst into song, in acknowledgment that it had a fraternal share in his joy (Ausubel 492).

One of the oldest Sabbath songs, sung in honor of the newly wedded youth, expressed the blessings that were held most dear—a loving companion, a long life spent in doing good, and a righteous posterity—and incorporated key principles which, if lived, would assure the new family unit a life of meaning and happiness.

Two of the most helpful and important insights relating to the interpretation of scriptural language follow. The fuller meanings in the Bridegroom Song can be discerned using these understandings.

Principle 1: *In Judaism, the citation of any part of a scripture text implied the whole context and not merely the quoted words* (Stern 27).

Thus, when a Jew heard a phrase in scripture that was also repeated in a different part of the Bible, he knew that those scriptures were tied together and had application for both texts.

For example, if the speaker quoted a phrase that contained a word from the Ten Commandments, it brought to the listener's mind the entire experience at Mt. Sinai when the Ten Commandments were received. This method of teaching and learning was like using a sort of verbal shorthand that the listener could expand in his own mind.

A secular example would be hearing someone repeat a portion of a well-known saying. "That's one small step for man..." would conjure up images of an excited and awed America that was seeing the heretofore impossible–a man on the moon. Additionally, the words could bring to mind a host of personal associations like the listener's age, location, and activity when the event occurred.

Of course, the phrase could be filled in mentally only by those who experienced, heard, later viewed, or read an account of the event. The deeper the background in American aeronautical history, the more significance those words had for the listener.

The Jews were thoroughly familiar with their history and prophetic sayings because those things were repeatedly read aloud on a regular basis. It was a common pattern for prophets to build on the foundation laid by earlier prophets. They did this by repeating significant words, phrases, and ideas and reinforcing them with their own message. A single word could link dozens of ideas together and give the listener much material to ponder. Every scripture could have dual meanings–personal and collective.

Principle 2: *Much of the Bible is written with symbols which have layers of meaning.*

There is a certain perspective, or way of viewing scriptural language that is very helpful. The symbolism of the wedding song can be viewed as a set of patterns and associations.

One writer said it so well:

> Biblical symbolism is not a code. It is instead a way of seeing, a perspective. For example, when Jesus speaks of "living water" (John 4:10), we rightly recog-

nize that He is using water as a symbol. We understand that when He spoke to the woman at the well, He was not merely offering her "water." He was offering her eternal life. *But He called it "water."* We should immediately ask: Why did He do that? He could have simply said "eternal life." Why did He speak in metaphor? Why did He want her to think of water?...When Jesus offered "water" to the woman, He wanted her to think of the multiple imagery connected with all forms of "water" in the Bible. In a general sense, of course, we know that water is associated with spiritual refreshment and sustenance of life...But Biblical associations with water are much more complex than that. This is *because understanding Biblical symbolism does not mean cracking a code.* It is much more like reading good poetry.

The symbolism of the Bible is not structured in a flat, this-means-that style. Instead, it is meant to be read visually. We are to *see* the images rise before us in succession, layer upon layer, allowing them to evoke a response in our *minds and hearts.*

So when the Bible tells us a story about water...we are expected to *see* the water and think of the Biblical associations with regard to water. What are some of the associations which might have occurred to the woman at the well and to the disciples? Here are a few of them:

1. The watery, fluid mass that was the original nature of the earth at the creation, and out of which God formed all life (Gen 1);
2. The great river of Eden that watered the whole earth (Gen. 2);
3. The salvation of Noah and his family by the waters of the Flood, out of which the earth was recreated (Gen. 6-9);
4. God's gracious revelations to Hagar by a fountain (Gen. 16) and a well (Gen. 21);
5. The well called Rehoboth, where God gave Isaac dominion (Gen. 26);
6. The river out of which the infant Moses, the

future Deliverer of Israel, was taken and made a prince (Ex. 2);
7. The redemptive crossing of the Red Sea, where God again saved His people by water (Ex. 14);
8. The water that flowed from the stricken Rock at Sinai, giving life to the people (Ex. 17);
9. The many ritual sprinklings in the Old Testament, signifying the removal of filth, pollution, sickness and death, and the bestowal of the Spirit upon the priests (e.g., Lev. 14; Num. 8);
10. The crossing of the Jordan River (Josh. 3);
11. The sound of rushing waters made by the pillar of cloud (Ezek. 1);
12. The River of Life flowing from the Temple and healing the Dead Sea (Ezek. 47).

Thus, when the Bible speaks of water, we are supposed to have in our mind a collection of associative concepts and images that affects our thinking about water. (Chilton 18-20)

To put it differently, "water" could be used as the modern equivalent of a "buzz-word", a term that calls to mind multiple associations and connotations. Whenever we read such terms, we can think of all the times when they are mentioned directly or are alluded to in scripture.

The wedding song written below is filled with many "buzz-words". The meanings of these terms will be used to explain how the creation of a new family in Israel brought the cycle of life to a full circle.

Sabbath Song For the Bridegroom

Rejoice O bridegroom, in the wife of your youth, your companion.
Let your heart be merry now, and when you shall grow old.
Sons to your sons shall you see: your old age's crown;
Sons who will prosper and work in place of their pious sires.
Your days in good shall be spent, your years in pleasantness.
Floweth your peace as a stream, riseth your worth as its waves.

The following listing of phrases and some of their associations is not intended to be exhaustive. Only a few can be mentioned. Hopefully, they will be instructive. (The song will be examined line by line.)

Rejoice O bridegroom in the wife of your youth, your companion.

These phrases especially echo two particular scriptures. The first is found in Proverbs 5:18:

> *Let thy* fountain *be blessed: and* rejoice in the wife of thy youth.

The sages taught that "the wife of your youth" held an inviolable position of love and value in her husband's heart. A wife surely was one of the greatest gifts a man could receive, and her presence was intended to be a continual reminder of divine generosity and blessing.

A *fountain* was sometimes used as a metaphor for refreshment of body and spirit. It was also symbolic of the life-giving capacity that a man and woman shared together. In Proverbs 5:15-18, there is a "highly poetic and beautiful exhortation" concerning marital fidelity and the blessings of posterity. True rejoicing was associated with the joyous anticipation of sharing in the blessings of Abraham, Isaac, and Jacob to have a posterity that would eventually be as numerous as the stars.

One additional source of *rejoicing* was the goodness of the Lord and his faithfulness in covenant keeping, His promises were always kept. When men (and women) were likewise faithful to every covenant they made, they earned the designation "perfect." In Jewish understanding, the Biblical sense of the word "perfect" did not mean flawless performance. To be "perfect" meant that one was faithful to covenants (Intrater 105). Unfaithfulness in covenant-keeping was harshly condemned, and most especially so when it concerned marital fidelity and family loyalty. The second related scripture, Malachi 2:14-16 states:

> *The Lord has been a witness between you and the* wife *of your youth, with whom ye have dealt treacherously [i.e. have broken covenant]; yet she is your companion and your wife by covenant. But did He not make them one?...And why one? He seeks godly offspring. Therefore, take heed to your spirit, and let none deal treacherously with* the *wife of his youth* (Hebrew translation).

The wife of one's youth points to faithfulness over the long period from youth to old age. It was in their *youth* that the couple would begin a family. This would fulfill God's stated purpose in marriage–to bring about godly offspring. The production of children who would follow in the footsteps of the covenant was immensely important. Biblical covenants depended on transgenerational commitment. They demanded a link by which covenants could be transferred to succeeding generations (Genesis 17:7). (Intrater 179)

Let your *heart be merry* now and when you shall *grow old.*
Being a member of the race chosen to have a covenant relationship with the only true and living God was a great privilege. To have that privilege plus a loving family would provide many occasions for gratitude and happiness. These feelings had a very positive effect upon physical and emotional health. In 2 Chronicles 7:10, we read how such gratitude affected the people when Solomon sent them home after the temple dedication:

> *...he sent the people away into their tents, glad and merry in heart for the goodness that the Lord had shewed...to Israel his people (KJV).*

The book of Proverbs lists more of the things associated with being *merry*. A merry heart was thought to do good for a person like a medicine (or tonic) and to cause the person who was merry to have a "continual feast" and a "cheerful countenance" (Proverbs 17:22; 15:15; and 15:13).

This blessing of a merry heart could continue even into old age. *Old age* and its accompanying virtues were highly desirable. In the Hebrew culture, the elderly were not downgraded, pushed aside, or made to feel superfluous. There was much to celebrate about old age. In a commentary on Exodus it states, "How welcome is old age! The aged are beloved by God." (Exodus Rabbah 5:12)

Of course, everyone expected physical capacities to diminish somewhat. There was a time for physical ability, and also a time to enjoy the privileges that age would bring. These times (and others) were clearly outlined:

> At five years old one is ready for the study of scriptures...at thirteen for the fulfilling of the commandments, at fifteen for the study of the Law, at eighteen for marriage, at twenty for the pursuit [of a livelihood], at thirty [man reaches] full strength, at forty full understanding, at fifty able to give counsel, at sixty for old age [i.e. for to be an elder–greatly respected], at seventy for gray hairs (a sign of blessing), at eighty [his survival reflects] special strength, at ninety for a bent body, and at one hundred he is as good as dead and passed away and ceased from the world (Abot 5:21).

In the Hebrew community of Bible times, gray (or white) hair was considered very beautiful (Proverbs 20:29) and was greatly desired as a "crown of splendor" (Proverbs 16:31). The Hebrews equated age with wisdom and experience. With gray hair came respect and honor: "Rise in the presence of the aged, show respect for the elderly, and revere your God. I am the LORD" (Leviticus 19:32). In the presence of gray hair, people of all ages stood silent, ready to be counseled in the way of wisdom. John fell on his face before the man with hair as "white as snow" (Revelation 1:14), an obvious pictorial allusion to the wisdom of the Lord (Wilson 230).

The elderly of those times did not desire to be passive, withdrawn, or merely relaxed. Those whose health permitted sought a style of life that was active, vigorous, and hard working.

In the New Testament, Simeon and Anna remained active in God's service at the Temple. Of Anna, a "very old" widow and prophetess...the Gospel of Luke says, "She departed not from the Temple, but served (worshipped) God with fasting and prayers night and day."

It is interesting to note that the Hebrew word *abad* meaning "to work", "to labor", and "to serve" is also translated "to worship". The fasting, faith, prayers, and temple worship of the elderly were types of "work" and "service" that blessed the entire community (Wilson 231).

Grandchildren were another reason for the elderly to be *merry*. Naomi was told that her grandson would be a great blessing to her:

> *And he shall be unto thee a restorer of [thy] life, and a nourisher of thine old age...* (Ruth 4:15a).

The next line of the wedding song continues this theme.

Sons to your sons shall you see, your old age's *crown*:
To see one's sons have sons of their own demonstrated the ideal of a long life and an extended posterity. Israelite prophets frequently used "trees" as symbols for the people because of their long lives, deep roots, and spreading branches. The roots represented ancestry and the branches typified posterity. To be cut off "root and branch" (Malachi 4:1) was a horrifying image because it meant no familial ties or increase. It was far better to be a "tree of life"–full of years, and still bearing fruit in old age. To be "fat and flourishing" to the end was a cherished symbol

and represented the desire of every Israelite. This blessing was firmly tied to the responsibility of the couple to be "planted in the house of the LORD" (Psalms 92:12-14). Through the sacrifices and covenants associated with the Temple, the blessings of a "good old age" could be realized.

There were two main types of *crowns* in ancient Israel; the crown of a King and the golden crown of the High Priest, which bore the inscription: HOLINESS TO THE LORD. The new husband would act in both roles—a king and a priest—by providing for the physical and spiritual needs of his family.

Earthly crowns were thought to be a type and shadow of the imperishable "crowns of righteousness" (2 Timothy 4:8) laid up in Heaven for the faithful. Crowns, glory, and posterity were frequently linked (Proverbs 17:6). The children of Israel were thought to be as "[precious] stones of a crown" treasured as the Lord's own possession.

There were two other symbolic "crowns" which were recognized as having significant importance. One was the crown of scholarship, which was possessed by those gifted with unusual intelligence. Their insights and deep understanding led to teachings which blessed many.

The other crown was called *shem tov* or a "good name". This crown was a good reputation and could be obtained by character development and service to the community. The crown of a good name and a worthy reputation was a valuable legacy to leave one's family.

Sons who will *prosper* and work in the place of their *pious* sires:

Moderation was considered desirable while pursuing material wealth and prosperity. To be too focused on earthly riches frequently led to pride, selfishness and ingratitude. But poverty was not held up as a desirable goal either. It was thought a blessing to be able to provide for one's own family, and to additionally have enough to help meet the needs of others less fortunate. But material prosperity was only one small aspect of what it meant Biblically to *prosper.*

A scripture search on the word "prosper" (or on a closely associated term, "be established" [2 Chronicles 20:20]) yields many helpful insights concerning how the ancient Hebrew prophets understood and taught this principle. The following is a brief summary of what the scriptures say about how one prospered, and what would keep Israel from prospering.

A collective scriptural definition includes three main elements:

1. Be blessed upon the land with *fruitfulness.* This meant that every material need would be met abundantly. Fruitfulness in this sense also encompassed ideas of kingdoms, crowns, glory, and posterity.
2. A *land of inheritance forever.* This referred to a place of safety and protection from all enemies.
3. Have *the Spirit of the Lord* to be with one continually. This gave the needed ability to fulfill all covenant commitments and to have peace and contentment.

True prosperity extended into the next life as well. To obtain these great blessings, a high standard was required. Here is a general list:

1. Make covenants with the Lord and keep them faithfully (Deut. 29:9);
2. Seek to be a holy people (Deut. 28:9);
3. Follow the Lord and His prophets (2 Chron. 20:20);
4. Seek the Lord (2 Chron. 31:21);
5. Be obedient (Gen. 39:3,23).

What would prevent one from obtaining these most desirable blessings? Again, the scriptures are plain about those behaviors and attitudes which are a deterrent to true prosperity:

1. Refuse to repent = not prosper.
2. Disobedience = not prosper.
3. Satisfaction with false *seeming* prosperity or putting trust in riches = not prosper.
4. Fight against God = not prosper.

Job 9:4 asks, "Who has hardened his heart against God and prospered?" This rhetorical question has an obvious answer–no one. It is clear that the ultimate prosperity was realized when one became worthy to enjoy the same covenant promises given to Abraham, Isaac, and Jacob. In the highest sense, these three forefathers comprised the main group of *pious sires*.

Your days in *good* shall be spent, your years in *pleasantness*:
Pleasantness and doing *good* were both associated with the qualities of *wisdom* mentioned in Proverbs 3:13-24. Wisdom was defined as the ability to see and evaluate all of life from God's point of view (Wilson 281).

In ancient times the Jews had special schools of Wisdom to train young students to develop *hokhmah* or practical wisdom, so that they could effectively cope with the problems of their society. In such schools, the teachers sought to instill in their students the virtues of hard work, moderation, seriousness, loyalty to authority and other elements of morality necessary for success. Students were admonished to constantly seek knowledge from all available sources: from books, from people, and from personal experience, so that they could become cultured people who could deal successfully with life's concerns and difficulties. Thus, they could be a blessing to the entire community (Glustrom 111-112).

Floweth your *peace* as a stream, riseth your worth as its waves.
The final line from the song expresses the wish dearest to the hearts of Israelite parents, the desire to have a *shalom bayit*, a

"peaceful home".

The ancient rabbis warned about the danger of bickering and controversy in the home: "Anger in the home is like worms in grain," and "A home where there is dissension will not stand."

To increase the level of peace, derogatory speech was forbidden. To encourage a positive and peaceful spirit, good deeds were often acknowledged with the blessing "more strength to you."

A *shalom bayit* was a home marked by the absence of strife. But *shalom bayit* was also a decidedly positive concept. The Hebrew word *shalom* is filled with strong and rich imagery. *Shalom* comes from a verb meaning "to be whole, sound, entire, well, complete, perfect". The rabbis often used *Shalom* as a name for God, in that he was the sum of perfection, and accordingly his Messiah was described as *sar shalom*, or "Prince of Peace" (see Isaiah 9:6). Furthermore, the Hebrew sense of *shalom* meant "to be in friendship, in right relations, and in harmony" with others—especially one's family. It also carried the idea of freedom from strife both externally and internally (Wilson 217-218).

But most essential, in a home where *shalom bayit* prevailed, husband and wife had great regard and respect for each other. There was a well-known saying about this matter:

> He who loves his wife as much as himself, honors her more than himself, and rears his children in the right manner, that man has peace in his household.

Since every home was considered Israel in microcosm, it was taught that if one brought envy and contention into his home, he was blamed for having brought envy and contention to Israel. And if one brought *peace* into his household, he received credit for bringing peace to all Israel.

CHAPTER TEN

Spiritual Betrothal

This chapter and the next one will explore the elements of wedding customs found in scripture, and will show how their fulfillment is found in Christ. The first part of the marriage was the *betrothal* or *erusin*. As found in Appendix I, there were seven elements to this process. Each of these elements will be listed and then pertinent associated scripture verses will be given.

BETROTHAL or ERUSIN

1. Choosing the Bride

Choosing a bride was the prerogative of the groom and his parents. The bride could only accept or reject the offer.

> *The LORD did not set his love upon you, nor choose you, because ye were more in number than any people, for ye were the fewest of all people* (Deuteronomy 7:7).

Only a "few"–the righteous remnant–will ultimately qualify to be chosen as a "bride". He chooses us because He loves us.

> *We love Him because* he first loved us (1 John 4:19).

We were loved and chosen by him from before the foundation of the world.

> *According as He hath chosen us in him* before the foundation of the world, *that we should be* holy, *and without blame before him in love* (Ephesians 1:4).

The root word for "holy" includes ideas of being sanctified, set apart, and consecrated. In this relationship, the Lord demands our exclusive devotion.

Parents generally chose the bride for their son. Abraham chose for Isaac:

> ...thou (Eliezar) shalt go unto my country, and to my kindred, and take (bring) a wife unto (for) my son Isaac (Genesis 24:4).

Hagar chose for Ishmael:

> And he dwelt in the wilderness of Paran: and his mother took him a wife out of the land of Egypt (Genesis 21:21).

Judah selected a wife for Er:

> And Judah took (chose) a wife for Er his firstborn, whose name was Tamar (Genesis 38:6).

Marriage came first, then love followed.

> And Isaac brought her into his mother Sarah's tent, and took Rebekah, and she became his wife; and (then) he loved her (Genesis 24:67).

2. The Proposal - Negotiation of the Bride Price

Brides were an acquired or purchased possession. The bride price was called the *mohar*. The word *mohar* is mentioned three times in the Old Testament.

> Ask of me a bride price ever so high, as well as gifts, and I will pay what you tell me; only give me the maiden for a wife (Genesis 34:12 [Hebrew trans.]).

> *If a man seduces a virgin for whom the bride price has not been paid, and lies with her, he must make her his wife by payment of a bride price* (Exodus 22:16 [v. 15 in Hebrew trans.]).

> *And Saul said, "Say this to David: 'The king desires no other bride price than the foreskins of a hundred Philistines"* (1 Samuel 18:25 [Tanakh]).

As noted above, service could sometimes be used in place of money to acquire a bride. This was also how Jacob acquired Rachel:

> *So Jacob served seven years for Rachel, and they seemed to him but a few days because of his love for her* (Genesis 29:20).

Christ paid the highest *mohar* possible for us. The high price shows how extremely valuable and precious we are to him.

> *Know ye not that your body is the temple of the Holy Ghost which is in you... and ye are not your own? For ye are bought with a price* (1 Corinthians 6:19-20).

> *Ye are bought with a price...* (1 Corinthians 7:23).

> *Take heed therefore unto yourselves and to all the flock, over the which the Holy Ghost hath made you overseers, to feed the Church of God, which he hath purchased with his own blood* (Acts 20:28).

The bride price for us was paid in installments. Christ's entire sinless life was lived so that he would be qualified to pay the ultimate price–his life. This was represented by the shedding of his blood–both at Gethsemane and on the cross.

At Gethsemane:

> *And he came out, and went...to the Mount of Olives; and his disciples also followed him. And when he was*

110 / SPIRITUAL BETROTHAL

> *at the place, he said unto them, Pray that ye enter not into temptation. And he was withdrawn from them about a stone's cast, and kneeled down, and prayed ...And being in agony he prayed more earnestly and his sweat was as it were great drops of blood falling down to the ground* (Luke 22:39-41,44).

Blood represented life and covenants. When the final installment of the *mohar* was being paid, it was three p.m. and Christ had been on the cross for six hours. In the temple at Jerusalem at three p.m., a horn was blown to announce that the final sacrifice of the day–a slaughtered lamb–had been completed.

> *And when Jesus had cried with a loud voice* ("It is finished." John 19:30), *he said, Father into thy hands I commend my spirit: And having said thus* ("...he bowed his head," John 19:30) *and gave up the ghost (i.e. his spirit)* (Luke 23:46, John 19:30).

After Christ finished paying the *mohar*, he said "It is finished." The phrase, "it is finished," is one word in both Hebrew and Greek. Both of those languages have wonderful nuances concerning this phrase which enhance our understanding.

In Hebrew, the word which he spoke as his final utterance is from the root *ka'lal*, which means "to complete," "to make perfect," "to finish," or "to consummate." It is from the same root as the word for bride: *kallah*. It is possible that Christ's words related to his most precious possession. Truly his "bride" was on his mind and in his heart.

> *...having loved his own which were in the world, he loved them unto the end* (John 13:1).

The Greek word for "it is finished" is *tetellestai*. This word had another connotation which sheds additional light on this. Anciently, for example, if a person committed a crime and received a prison sentence, that sentence was written on a piece of parchment and hung by the door of their cell. Every day that the sentence was served was marked off. When the time had been served and every debt paid, the jailer would then write across the paper, "*tetellestai,*" which meant "paid in full." In other words, Christ had paid the bride price in full. In one older hymn, *The Church's One Foundation*, there is a verse which beautifully portrays this understanding concerning the Church as a bride:

> From Heaven He came and sought her
> To be his holy bride
> With his own blood he bought her
> And for her life, he died. (Samuel J. Stone)

3. A marriage contract - *ketuba* - was given to the bride which listed the promises of the bridegroom.

This marriage contract was totally one-sided, stating what he would do for *her*, what he would give *her*, and how he would care and provide for *her*. The bride did not have to do anything or make any promises. All she had to do was accept his promises willingly and with the intent of faithfulness. The bride from that time would turn her back on any other suitors and her life would be totally devoted to their relationship. She was to have no one else before him. He claimed first place in her heart and loyalty. Of course, unfaithfulness on her part would void the contract and cause the loss of her promised blessings.

The first condition of the *ketuba* was that the groom promised to provide his bride with food, clothing, and necessities. The Lord gave this promise also.

> *The Lord is concerned for the needs of the blameless; their portion lasts forever; they shall not come to grief in bad times;(even) in famine, they shall eat their fill.... I have been young and am now old, but I have never seen a righteous man abandoned, or his children begging bread* (Psalm 37:18, 25 Tanakh).

> *And why be anxious about* clothing? *Think about the fields of wild irises and how they grow...not even Solomon in all his glory was clothed as beautifully as one of these....Won't He much more* clothe you? *What little trust you have! So don't be anxious, asking, "What will we eat?" "What will we drink?" or "How will we be clothed?"*
>
> *...Your Heavenly Father knows you need all these things. But seek first his kingdom and His righteousness and all these things will be given to you as well* (Matthew 6:28-31,33 JNT).

We can claim his promises through our trust in Him and our faithfulness in covenant keeping.

The second stipulation of the *ketuba* was that the Bridegroom promised to redeem the bride if she were ever taken captive. As a people, we all have fallen short and are under spiritual bondage and captivity.

> *For all have sinned, and come short of the glory of God* (Romans 3:23).

> *Jesus answered them, Verily, verily, I say unto you, whosoever commiteth sin is the servant of sin* (John 8:34).

Go'el was the term used for a redeemer who was a near kinsman (see Leviticus 25:48-49). Christ was willing to become "related" to us–as a near kinsman–by taking upon himself a body of flesh and blood so that he could give his life to ransom us.

> *As for our redeemer, the Lord of Hosts is his name, the Holy One of Israel* (Isaiah 47:4).

> *Forasmuch as the children (of men) are partakers of flesh and blood, he also himself took part of the same; that through death he might destroy him that had the power of death, that is, the devil; and deliver them who through fear of death were all their lifetime subject to bondage* (Heb. 2:14-15).

> *And he will take upon him death, that he may loose the bands of death which bind the people...*(Alma 7:12).

Sin creates a debt to eternal law and justice that we cannot repay. Each of us needs a redeemer, a near kinsman who is willing and able to pay the price to ransom us from bondage.

> *For thus saith the LORD, ye have sold yourselves for nothing; and ye shall be redeemed without money* (Isaiah 52:3).

A modern Jewish believer in Christ has written a helpful explanation concerning the Hebrew connection between paying a ransom and blood:

> In 1 Samuel 14, Jonathan came under sentence of death for transgressing a public oath his father made in his absence. Yet although King Saul condemned him to die, the sentence was not carried out, because the people objected. But law is law, not to be ignored. So they ransomed him, and thus legally prevented his being put to death. We too, like Jonathan, have come under the sentence of death. Jonathan was condemned to death even though he had been unaware of King Saul's oath and order. We are condemned to death even though we have not sinned after the manner of the first Adam (see Romans 5:12-14). Like Jonathan, we must either die or be ransomed.
> Jonathan and the Israel firstborn were ransomed with money. Money equals blood. One of the names for money in Hebrew is *damim*, plural of *dam*, blood, because it represents man's labor and risks. It is a Mishnaic term. But money cannot redeem from eternal death. Man has nothing with which to ransom himself or others (Psalm 49:7-9); God himself must redeem him from the power of the grave (Psalm 49:15). But of God it is written, "I have found a ransom" (Job 33:24); and that ransom is the blood of the Messiah (cited in JNTC 578).

The third and last promise in the *ketuba* was the groom's promise to live as a husband with the bride and to give her an opportunity to bear children. In Hebrew "to bear children" was synonymous with the term "to bear fruit." Children were called the "fruit of the womb (Luke 1:42)." One wedding psalm (Psalm 128) used this example:

> *Thy wife shall be as the* fruitful vine *upon the walls of thine house* (v. 3).

The vine was a normal metaphor for Israel, the Bride (Psalms 80:8-14; Isaiah 5:1-7; Jeremiah 2:21; Hosea 10:1). Christ strongly stressed his union with Israel—so much so that he termed himself a vine also. Indeed, he is the True Vine.

> *I am the vine, ye are the branches: He that abideth in me, and I in him, the same bringeth forth* much fruit: *for without me ye can do nothing* (John 15:5).

Our union with Christ causes us to bear the fruit of good works and the fruits of the Spirit. The law of God is to be taken from outside of us and placed inside—in our hearts—that we might come *to know* and love the giver of the law. In Hebrew the word "know" is "*yada.*" It implies the superlative sense of intimate knowledge.

> *But this shall be the covenant that I will make with the house of Israel...I will put my law in their inward parts, and write it in their hearts; and will be their God, and they shall be my people. And they shall teach no more every man his neighbor, and every man his brother saying, Know the LORD: for they shall all know me, from the least of them to the greatest of them*...(Jeremiah 31:33-34).

4. A gift or gifts of value were offered to the Bride.
These gifts demonstrated a willingness to sacrifice and were a reminder of the bridegroom's devotion. In the ancient Middle

East, the gift was considered to be an actual extension of himself and established his authority over the bride; it had to be his own possession–free and clear.

As we have already seen concerning the *ketuba*, Christ gave us the gift of *redemption*. This was a free gift to us but was acquired at the cost of great sacrifice on his part. *Only someone who was completely free could redeem another.* Christ had the necessary power to redeem us because he was totally free. Since Christ had never broken his covenants with his Father, Satan had no power or control over him.

In John 14:30-31, the Savior bears witness of this to his disciples:

> *I won't be talking with you much longer, because the ruler of this world is coming. He has no claim on me; rather, this is happening so that the world may know that I love the Father and that I do as the Father has commanded me* (JNT).

The bride desired the Bridegroom's gifts because by adorning herself with them, she hoped to enhance her beauty in his eyes.

Some of the gifts we can enjoy are the Holy Spirit (Acts 2:38), faith, wisdom, knowledge, healing, and prophecy (1 Corinthians 12:8-11), and every other spiritual gift. The Sabbath day is also one of His gifts. The Bridegroom wants to delight his bride with his present (and presence!), and it comes with a promise:

> *If you refrain from trampling the Sabbath, from pursuing your affairs on my holy day;*
> *If you call the Sabbath "delight," The LORD's holy day "honored";*
> *If you honor it and go not your ways nor look to your affairs, nor strike bargains;*
> *Then you can seek the favor of the LORD. I will set you astride the heights of the earth, and let you enjoy the heritage of your father Jacob; For the mouth of the LORD has spoken* (Isaiah 58:13-14 Hebrew trans.).

The Sabbath has always been a day of rest to the Jews—a mortal foretaste of the rest Israel will find in the future Millennial days with her Messiah—and a time of great peace and happiness. One Hebrew word for "rest" means "security in the house of a husband." This sense is used in Ruth 1:9 and 3:1. The gift of "rest" is also shown in the promises of Christ given in Matthew 11:28:

> Come unto me, all ye that labor and are heavy laden, and I will give you rest.

In 1 Corinthians 11:24, we read of another gift given us by the Bridegroom:

> And when he had given thanks, he brake it (the bread), and said, Take, eat: this is my body which is broken for you. This do in remembrance of me.

The last night that Christ spent with his disciples was during Passover, a beautiful feast celebrated by the Jews to commemorate their deliverance from Egypt, slavery, and death. The Passover meal had several elements, the main one being roasted lamb. The lamb was prepared according to very strict specifications. The lamb had to pass an exacting inspection by the priests, so that it was found to have no fault or blemish. It had to be roasted whole in an upright position, and this was done by making a stand with branches from a pomegranate tree lashed together in the shape of the ancient Hebrew letter Tav (+). The lamb was roasted in an especially constructed oven. It was forbidden to break any bones of the roasted sacrificial lamb.

Every Passover was a covenant meal—always reminding Israel that her God would ever deliver her in her troubles if she were faithful to her covenant. All Israelites who kept the law ate of the lamb which was slain.

While Christ was on the cross, John tells us that for religious reasons, the Jews besought Pilate that his legs, and

BELOVED BRIDEGROOM / 117

those crucified with him, might be broken. However, to show a fulfillment of Christ as the True Passover Lamb, verse 33 of John 19 tells us that:

When they came to Jesus and saw that he was dead already, they brake not his legs.

Anciently, David had prophesied:

He keepeth all his bones: not one of them is broken(Psalms 34:20).

What gift then, did the *broken* bread represent? The next verse in John continues:

But one of the soldiers with a spear pierced his side, and forthwith there came out blood and water (John 19:34).

In the Journal of the American Medical Association (JAMA) 21 March 1986, there is a medical analysis of the crucifixion. In it, the doctors conclude that the blood and water that poured out after the soldier's sword was thrust in his side was an indication that the largest factor in Christ's death was a cardiac rupture; in other words, a *broken heart*.

This was his supreme gift offered to us as the prospective bride, and we are reminded of it every time we partake of the sacrament bread. Only with an open, humble, and receptive heart can we fully appreciate and receive this great gift. Little wonder then that to show our grateful devotion and mutual commitment, he asks for a similar sacrifice on our part.

Thou shalt offer a sacrifice unto the Lord thy God in righteousness, even that of a broken heart and a contrite spirit (Doctrine and Covenants 59:8).

5. Acceptance and Consent of Bride
The proposal had been made, the bride price determined, and a gift of value offered.

It was at this point that a cup of wine was placed before the bride. The bride's willing consent was vital for the transaction to be completed. This willing consent in Hebrew is *daat*. It is consent which comes from the heart. Judaism teaches that marriage can only take place by mutual consent. In an age when very young marriages were a common practice, the leaders ruled that: "It is forbidden for a man to betroth his minor daughter until she attains her majority (legal age) and says, *I love this man* (i.e. I will marry him)" (Lash 12). There could be no coercion.

Like the ancient Jewish bride, we have our free will and can choose to either accept or reject the terms offered to us by our Savior. We choose whether or not we are willing to accept the new (marriage) covenant which he freely gives us.

If the bride drank from the cup which was placed before her, she signaled her willingness to take upon herself the name of her groom and all that name represented. She was accepting a covenant relationship with serious implications. If she were unfaithful, curses would befall her (1 Corinthians 11:26-30). If faithful, however, this covenant would be a source of eternal blessing.

> ...*I would that ye should* take upon you the name of Christ, *all you that have entered into the covenant with God that ye should be obedient unto the end of your lives. And it shall come to pass that whosoever doeth this shall be found at the right hand of God, for he shall know the name by which he is called; for he shall be called by the name of Christ* (Mosiah 5:8-9).

The bride and her groom shared the same name after making a covenant together. We see an example of this in Jeremiah 23:6 and 33:16:

> In his (the Messiah's) days Judah shall be saved, and Israel shall dwell safely: and this is his name whereby he shall be called, THE LORD OUR RIGHTEOUSNESS.

> *In those days, Judah shall be saved,* and *Jerusalem shall dwell safely: and this is the name wherewith she shall be called,* The LORD our righteousness.

According to Biblical understanding, the bestowal of a name was a sacred trust and act. One's name spoke of identity, tradition, commitment, and membership in the covenant. "To honor a name" was not only to be true to one's self, but also to that tradition for which the name stood (Torah Commentary 119).

Another element sometimes figured in the bride's consent. For example, in the case of Rebekah, the bride did not see the groom beforehand. But she trusted in the description of his servant or servants and accepted the proposal. We have the same opportunity.

> *Whom having not seen, ye love; in whom, though now ye see him not, yet believing, ye rejoice with joy unspeakable and full of glory: receiving the end of your faith, even the salvation of your souls* (1 Peter 1:8).

We see our Bridegroom through the eyes of faith now. One day we will see Him face to face.

6. Ritual Statement and Consecration

The groom made a ritual statement to his new bride after she drank from the "cup of covenant." He spoke words similar to these, "Thou art set apart (or consecrated) for me according to the law of Moses and Israel."

Both the Hebrew and Greek words that refer to a person who has been "set apart" are ordinarily translated as "saint." A saint can be defined Biblically as an individual with a holy purpose—one who lives a life devoted to Christ. In this sense, every "saint" is like a bride who has made serious covenants and is obliged to be completely faithful to her covenant partnership.

As God's covenant people, Israel was "a holy (set apart, sanctified, consecrated) people...above all people that are upon the face of the earth (Deuteronomy 7:6)."

After accepting the covenant terms, the bride was unfaithful if she loved anyone or anything more than her covenant partner. Such unfaithfulness was viewed as spiritual adultery. The word for "adultery" in Hebrew (Strong 5003) also has the figurative understanding of "apostasy." A "wicked and an adulterous generation" described a covenant group who were false-hearted and unfaithful in deed and thought.

Like all loving bridegrooms, the Lord gave Israel—his bride—an endearing name. We find it in Exodus 19:5

> *Now then, if you will obey me faithfully and keep my covenant, you shall be my* treasured possession (KJV *"peculiar treasure") among all the people.*

7. Witnesses

A minimum of two witnesses was required for every covenant agreement. The "friend of the bridegroom" was generally one of the witnesses at the time the betrothal was completed. The witnesses were required to oversee the signing of the *ketuba* by both parties and also the giving of the gift of value. They listened to the bridegroom's ritual statements and witnessed the bride's acceptance by drinking the cup of wine.

When a covenant relationship was established between the Lord and the children of Israel, Moses called for the elders of the people to witness the completion of the covenantal transaction. This is found in Exodus 19:7-8,

> *And Moses came and called for the elders of the people, and laid before their faces all these words which the Lord commanded \them. And the people answered together, and said, All that the LORD hath spoken, we will do. And Moses returned the words of the people unto the LORD.*

In essence, their declaration was also an acceptance of the blessings and implied cursings given in the Law. The ten commandments are a type for the *ketuba*.

From then on Israel had the designation *me'kudeshet*—one who was betrothed, sanctified, and dedicated to her Bridegroom. Each commandment Israel kept in the right spirit was an act of loving God.

From this point on, to break the Law established between Israel and God would be like the breaking of a marriage vow. It meant that all unfaithfulness to Him—all sin—was a "sin against love." Such disloyalty would break his heart.

CHAPTER ELEVEN

Spiritual Preparation and Marriage

With the betrothal or *erusin* phase completed, the bridegroom and his bride would begin their mutual preparations for their future life together. This second stage–from betrothal to consummation–was collectively called *nissu'in*. The components of this period are listed below.

PREPARATION FOR MARRIAGE

A. Groom's Responsibilities and Friend's Duties

The bridegroom's first task was to prepare a nuptial chamber or new home for his bride. This was done under the supervision of his father. It was often attached to a family compound where several other families also lived.

When the father gave his approval of the new dwelling, the bridegroom could go and get his new bride and bring her to his father's house. The father was the one who determined that time.

> *Let not your heart be troubled: ye believe in God, believe also in me, In my Father's house are many mansions: if it were not so I would have told you. I go to prepare a place for you* (John 14:1-2).

> *But of that day and hour [the Bridegroom's return] knoweth no man, no not the angels of heaven, but my Father only* (Matthew 24:36).

While the bridegroom was away–preparing a place for his bride–the "friend of the groom" would act as a liaison between them. He could pass messages, deliver additional gifts, watch over her chastity, and comfort and reassure the bride that her groom would surely return.

> *Nevertheless, I tell you the truth; it is expedient for you that I go away: for if I go not away, the Comforter will not come unto you; but if I depart, I will send him unto you...when he, the Spirit of truth is come, he will guide you into all truth: for he shall not speak of himself; but whatsoever he shall hear, that shall he speak: and he will show you things to come. He shall glorify me: for he shall receive of mine and show it unto you* (John 16:7, 13-14).

Barclay shares a helpful insight which enriches our understanding about the role of the Comforter:

> So then the Holy Spirit is the person through whom there comes to us the strength and grace of God to enable us to cope with life. Certainly, part of this work is to comfort, but only part. To call the Holy Spirit the Comforter, and to stop there, is to have a limited and rather sentimental view of the Spirit, whereas in the Greek the word is full of power and of the promise of the God-given ability to face and to master any situation in life.
> How then did this word Comforter get into the English translation of the Bible? It came in with Wycliffe about 1386, and it has stayed ever since. But in the days of Wycliffe it was a perfect translation. The word *comfort* is derived from the Latin word *fortis*, which means *brave*, and originally the word meant someone who puts courage into you. Let us take two other examples of it in Wycliffe. Wycliffe translates **Ephesians 6:10** as, "Be ye *comforted* in the Lord." And he translates 1 Timothy 1:12, "I do thanksgiving to him who *comforted* me." In both cases the word in the Greek is *endunamoun*, whose root word is *dunamis*, power, from which the word *dynamite* comes. In Wycliffe's day to *comfort* a person was to fill that person with a power like spiritual dyn-

amite. The Holy Spirit does not simply come and wipe our tears away; he gives us a dynamic power to cope with life (*Introducing the Bible* 117).

John the Baptist was the earthly "friend of the bridegroom" for Jesus. Others in scripture have also earned this title by their faithfulness, commitment, and service to the covenant people of the Lord–His "bride." It is a title of great honor and trust.

> *And the LORD spake unto Moses face to face, as a man speaketh unto his* friend (Exodus 33:11a).

> *And the scripture was fulfilled which saith, Abraham believed God, and it was imputed to him for righteousness: and he was called the* Friend of God (James 2:23).

Paul and the other disciples and Apostles acted in the role of "friend." Christ told them:

> *Ye are my friends, if ye do whatsoever I command you. Henceforth, I call you not servants; for the servant knoweth not what his lord doeth: but I have called you friends; for all things that I have heard of my Father I have made known unto you* (John 15:14-15).

Paul told us of his feelings concerning this weighty assignment,

> *For I am jealous over you [the Church] with Godly jealousy: for I have espoused you to one husband, that I may present you as a chaste virgin to Christ* (2 Corinthians 11:2).

B. Preparation of the Consecrated Bride

When Israel was betrothed to God at Sinai, she was commanded to cleanse herself with a *mikvah*. This is symbolically represented in Exodus 19:10:

> *And the Lord said unto Moses, Go unto the people, and sanctify them today and tomorrow, and have them wash their clothes.*

Not only their bodies, but their clothing–their garments–were washed. Brides in ancient times went to a *mikvah* before marriage. As discussed in Chapter Eight, a *mikvah* was a ritual immersion in "living water." It symbolized many things. Besides representing a preparation for holiness, it also represented a separation from an old life to a new life–from life as a single woman to life as a married woman. It also symbolized a change in status and authority; a woman came out from under the authority of her father to the authority of her husband (Lash 18).

Water immersion was a type for the more complete cleansing that came from the Holy One of Israel. A rabbi from the first century taught:

> Who cleanses you from your transgressions? Your Father in Heaven....It also says *Mikvah-Israel* [which can be translated either "the hope of Israel" or "the ritual immersion of Israel" (Jeremiah 17:13). Just as a ritual bath cleanses the unclean, so does the Holy One, blessed be he, cleanse Israel (Rabbi Akiva - Yoma 8:8-9 cited in JNTC 770).

Our bodies and our clothing both need to be washed and kept clean to make us fit covenant companions. Jesus Christ is our "hope"–our "*Mikvah-Israel*"–and he can sanctify and cleanse us in every needful way.

> *That he might sanctify and cleanse it [the Church] with the washing of water by the word* (Ephesians 5:26 KJV).

> *In order to set it apart for God, making it clean through immersion in the* mikvah, *so to speak* (Ephesians 5:26 JNT).

> *...for there can no man be saved except his garments are washed white; yea, his garments must be purified until they are cleansed from all stain, through the blood of him of whom it has been spoken by our fathers, who should come to redeem his people from their sins* (Alma 5:21).

Baptism by water was essential. Mark 16:16 says:

> He that believeth and is baptized shall be saved [another word for redeemed]...

Our *Mikvah-Israel* can make us clean through His atoning sacrifice which gives us true *hope*.

> *...ye shall have* hope *through the atonement of Christ and the power of his resurrection, to be raised unto life eternal, and this because of your faith in him according to the promise* (Moroni 7:41).

A consecrated bride would concern herself with the matters which most interested her new husband. She would spend her time, energy, and resources in ways that would honor him.

> *And after you have obtained a hope in Christ...ye will...do good—to clothe the naked, and to feed the hungry, and to liberate the captive, and to administer relief to the sick and afflicted* (Jacob 2:19).

The bride's righteous actions would signify that she was using one of the "gifts of value" given to her—the scriptures—to learn how to make herself beautiful for Him. Such purity and goodness would make her truly lovely in His eyes.

A betrothed bride also wore some special items of clothing which set her apart. A modern author has written about some of this clothing:

> In the east, you can easily tell the religion of many people by the clothes they wear. Just as the Sadducees and Pharisees were known by their phylacteries and

fringes, today's Sikhs and Buddhist priests are also identified by turbans and saffron robes. Christ's bride has been clothed with garments that mark us, too. One of these is the clothing of power that was promised in Luke 24:49, that great enabling which the Holy Spirit grants us [note: "endued" means clothed or invested]. Perhaps we could more accurately term it an undergarment or foundation, for though it is not usually visible to outsiders, it is an essential part of our spiritual wardrobe (Greenwood 69).

In Revelation 19:8, we read about the outer clothing that is worn by the bride. She is dressed in "fine linen—clean and white." Thus attired with good deeds, she is truly "dressed for success" in the highest and eternal sense.

The veil covering her hair was a symbol of modesty in dress, action, and speech. It was worn by the bride to show that she had been "set apart for holiness." In our culture today, an engagement ring gives the same message. The ring is a gift treasured by the bride. Because it represents both monetary value and personal sentiment, she would not be careless with her diamond. The ring, like the veil, was a special sign to all who saw her.

Another special sign was also given by the Bridegroom to His bride:

> Moreover, also, I gave them my Sabbaths, to be a sign between me and them, that they might know that I am the LORD that sanctify them (Ezekiel 20:12).

When Israel did not honor this gift and sign (the Sabbath) between her and her LORD, she polluted her gift and violated her *ketuba* through unfaithfulness. This was seen as spiritual adultery and caused her to lose great blessings.

> Because they despised my judgments and walked not in my statutes, but polluted my sabbaths: for their heart went after their idols (Ezekiel 20:16).

A bride would speak often of her Beloved, especially when she was with her close companions. Remember that "companion" means "one with whom bread is broken." What better time to remember covenant promises and think of Jesus Christ than while partaking of the emblems of the Sacrament?

> *And there was one day in every week that was* set apart *that they should gather themselves together to teach the people and to worship the Lord their God...* (Mosiah 18:25).

It is worth noting that the Sabbath was set apart from the rest of the week. This is one reason that the Jews call the Sabbath a bride. Samuel H. Dresner tells us more concerning this title:

> Why is the Sabbath called a bride? What does the term symbolize? The symbol of a bride is love, devotion, and joy—an inward feeling. It is this peculiar inward feeling...which characterizes the Sabbath day. (To the Jew) the Sabbath is a bride. Just as one prepares for a bride with the utmost care and meticulous detail, so the Sabbath is preceded by careful preparation. Just as one yearns for the arrival of a bride, so is the Sabbath met and welcomed. Just as the presence of a bride elicits tender concern, so does the Sabbath evoke love and devotion. Just as the departure of a bride occasions sadness, so is the departure of the Sabbath.... In all ways, she is the *Shabbat Ha Kallah*, the Sabbath Bride.

The author continues in a slightly different vein:

> The Sabbath is a bride and its celebration is like a wedding....There is a hint of this in the Sabbath prayers. In the evening service we say *Thou hast sanctified the seventh day,* referring to the marriage of the bride to the groom (sanctification–*kiddushin*–is the Hebrew word for marriage). In the morning prayer

we say *Moses rejoiced in the gift* [of the Sabbath] bestowed upon him which corresponds to the groom's rejoicing with the bride. In prayer we make mention of *the two lambs, the fine flour for a meal offering mingled with oil and the drink thereof,* referring to the meat, the bread, the wine, and the oil used in the wedding banquet. In the last hour of the day we say *Thou art One,* to parallel the consummation of the marriage by which the bride and groom are united.

As a note of interest, there is a very old Sabbath song sung in many Jewish homes called "The Rock From Which We Have Eaten." It contains the idea that the manna (bread from Heaven) and the water (which poured forth from the rock which Moses struck) gave *spiritual* as well as physical nourishment. The bread and water given to Israel in the desert was especially blessed for the good of their *souls*. Here are two stanzas from the song:

> The Rock, from whom we have eaten–
> Bless him, my faithful friends!
> We have eaten our fill without exhausting the supply,
> Which accords with the words of *Adonai*.
>
> He nourishes his world, our Shepherd, our Father;
> We have eaten his bread, and drunk his wine...
> With nourishment and sustenance *he has sated our souls...*
> May the Merciful One be blessed and Exalted! (469-70 JNTC)

Truly the Sabbath was a gift, which if honored, would help the bride come to better know, love, and appreciate her Bridegroom. It was a glorious foretaste of the Millennial day of peace and rest.

WEDDING or NISSU'IN

1. With the Father's Approval, the Son Could Go and Take His Bride.

When the wedding house was finished, it was thoroughly inspected by the groom's father. The father desired to be well represented by his son. To follow the Son's example, and also please our Heavenly Father, we should likewise work hard and study to show ourselves approved. We can strive to present ourselves as someone worthy of His approval, able to meet the highest standards of quality. Of course, this will require much thought and effort on our part, but His approbation will be ample reward for all our hard work.

> *Do all you can to present yourself to God as someone worthy of his approval, as a worker with no need to be ashamed, because he deals straightforwardly with the word of the Truth* (2 Timothy 2:15 JNT).

The bridegroom would gather his friends together to go and take his new bride. Christ made this promise:

> *If I go and prepare a place for you, I will come again and receive you unto myself; that where I am, there ye may be also* (John 14:3).

The group would come carrying torches that would shine brightly in the dark night, comparable to lightning in the Middle Eastern mind:

> *For as lightning cometh out of the east and shineth even unto the west, so shall also the coming of the Son of Man be* (Matthew 24:27).

2. Bride and Her Attendants

As shown in the Parable of the Ten Virgins, the exact day and hour was not known to the bride and her attendants—only the groom's father knew specifically.

> But of that day and hour knoweth no man, no, not the angels of heaven, but my Father only (Matthew 24:36). [For a fascinating discussion on "the hidden day" see *The Seven Festivals of the Messiah* by Edward Chumney 130-131]

The "friend of the bridegroom" would, of course, keep the anxious bride updated on the groom's progress and the approximate time of his return. A wise bride and her companions had their oil lamps filled, their light shining, and their clothing prepared, anticipating his estimated time of arrival based on his friend's messages. To those who were foolish and slothful, his arrival would be as "a thief in the night."

> *For yourselves know perfectly that the day of the Lord cometh as a thief in the night. But ye...are not in darkness, that the day should overtake you as a thief. Ye are all the children of light, and the children of the day: we are not of the night, nor of darkness. Therefore, let us not sleep, as do others; but let us watch and be sober....Let us who are of the day be sober, putting on the breastplate of faith and love....Wherefore, comfort yourselves together, and edify one another...*(1 Thessalonians 5:2, 4-6, 8, 11).

As the above scripture mentions, the "children of the light" are like the waiting wise virgins. Wise virgins would spend their time productively—wearing appropriate clothing (for example, the breastplate of faith and love) and would gather together as supportive friends and family who would edify and comfort one another. This would help them to continue trusting in the Bridegroom's return, while remaining grounded and steady.

In the parable, a short time before his arrival at the bride's home, a shout was given by those in the procession with the groom. This gave her time to quickly prepare and dress. A short time later—never more than half an hour—he arrived. Perhaps this time period is also referenced in scripture:

> And there shall be silence in heaven for the space of half an hour [after the seventh seal is opened Revelation 8:1]; and immediately after shall the curtain of heaven be unfolded...and the face of the Lord shall be unveiled (Doctrine and Covenants 88:95).

The bridegroom had come to take his bride to her new home. The bride was "lifted up" in her *aperion* (bridal chair) and carried by several strong men who were called *Giborei Yisrael* or the Heroes of Israel.

There are poignant types for us to ponder in this example. Like the bride, Christ was also "lifted up," but his lifting up was on the cross.

> And as [Moses] lifted up the brazen serpent in the wilderness, even so shall he be lifted up who shall come (Helaman 8:14).

Because of this sacrifice, as we prove patient and faithful, even in trials, we shall have a great blessing:

> ...the Lord seeth fit to chasten his people; yea, he trieth their patience and their faith. Nevertheless—whosoever putteth his trust in him the same shall be lifted up at the last day (Mosiah 23:21-22).

The bride was carried in comfort, because she bore the name of her new lord.

> Yea, blessed is this people because they are willing to bear my name; for in my name shall they be called; and they are mine. (Mosiah 26:18)

In Isaiah 53 verses 4 and 11 we learn what our Bridegroom had to bear so that he could claim us as his own:

> *Surely, he hath* borne our griefs, *and* carried our sorrows: ...*He shall see the* travail *of his soul and shall be satisfied: by his knowledge shall my righteous servant justify many; for he shall* bear their iniquities.

This was an extremely painful experience. In the Bible, "travail" was the word for childbirth. Christ's atoning sacrifice was literally a giving of life to his bride at a cost of great personal suffering. It is interesting to know that the Jews believed that it would take "*Chevlai shel Mashiach*" or the "Birth pangs of the Messiah" to bring to pass redemption.

> Just as birth is preceded and accompanied by birth pangs, there are likewise "pangs of Messiah" in the generation in which the Son of David will appear (Schneerson 161).

Isaiah 42:14 uses a simile of Jehovah experiencing labor pains:

> *From the beginning, I have been silent, I have kept quiet, held myself in check, I groan like a woman in labor, I suffocate, I stifle* (JB, emphasis added).

Powerfully, God's anguish at the human failure to embody justice is captured in the image of a woman writhing, unable to catch her breath in the pain of her travail....But out of this travail comes a new world in which the blind are safely led, their darkness turning to light as shown in Isaiah 42:16 (Mollenkott 15).

Surely, our Bridegroom is the greatest of all of the "Heroes of Israel" for the burden he carried was incredible.

> *And he shall go forth, suffering pains and afflictions and temptations of every kind...he will take upon him the pains and the sicknesses of his people. And he will take upon him death, that he may loose the bands of death which bind his people; and he will take upon him their infirmities, that his bowels may be filled with mercy ...that he may know according to the flesh how to succor his people according to their infirmities* (Alma 7:11-12).

In Hebrew, the word for mercy or compassion, *rachum* or *racham*, is closely related to the word for womb—*rechem* or *racham* (Strong 7356). Mercy was thought to be the same kind of compassion that a mother would show for the child of her womb. Perhaps the mercy that Christ showed was related to his sufferings in the garden and on the cross which brought forth new life for all who would repent and accept Him.

He used a birth image to comfort his disciples concerning the difficulties they would confront. In John 16:21 he told them that a woman had sorrow when her *hour was come* and her birth contractions began, but her sorrow would later turn to joy by the actual arrival of the baby. According to John's account it was only minutes later that Jesus began to pray with the words, "Father, *the hour is come* (17:1). What hour? The hour of travail—of pain and sorrow" (Mollenkott 17).

But thank heavens, the sorrow was turned to joy—both for Christ and also for us. Because of him, we are redeemed, and Zion is the type for that ultimate home to which our Heavenly Bridegroom will bring us. There will be a great and joyful procession:

> *Therefore, the redeemed of the LORD shall return, and come with singing unto Zion; and everlasting joy shall be upon their head: they shall obtain gladness and joy; and sorrow and mourning shall flee away* (Isaiah 51:11).

3. Arrival of the Bridal Pair

Upon arrival at the home of the bridegroom's father, both bride and groom were welcomed and blessed. Their feet were washed, and they were anointed, and dressed in their wedding clothing. Psalm 45 recounts the arrival and welcome of the bridal pair. By the time of Christ, Psalm 45 had a spiritual interpretation along with its royal marriage associations.

> This psalm came to be understood as referring to King Messiah, and his marriage as an allusion to the redemption of Israel (Stern 666).

The psalm describes some of the nuptial apparel:

> (Groom) *Thy God hath anointed thee with the oil of gladness (generally associated with olive oil)...all thy garments [are fragrant] with myrrh and aloes and cassia* (Psalm 45:7-8).

> (Bride) *The royal princess, her dress embroidered with golden mountings, is led inside to the King. Maidens in her train, her companions, are presented to you. They are led in with joy and gladness; they enter the palace of the king* (Psalm 45:13-14 Hebrew trans.).

In Revelation 19:7-8, we find another example of the bride's clothing.

> *Let us be glad and rejoice, and give honor to him: for the marriage of the Lamb is come, and his wife hath made herself ready. And to her was granted that she should be arrayed in fine linen, clean and white...*

The groom wore his *kittel*—a white coat girded with a white sash. It was a symbol of purity and solemn joy—a robe of righteousness and a garment of salvation.

4. The Wedding Canopy

There was a sacred procession where the bridegroom was led to the *huppah* (marriage canopy) first, there to welcome his bride. As he approached the canopy, the guests chanted, "Blessed is he who comes." Christ said that he would not return for his bride until these words were said.

> *For I say into you, Ye shall not see me henceforth, till ye shall say, Blessed is he that cometh in the name of the Lord* (Matthew 23:39).

There were two cups of wine that were shared by the couple under the *huppah*. The first was the "cup of joy." The second had two names: the "cup of sacrifice" and "the cup of salvation."

Christ also drank from a cup for us, although the order was reversed for him. He had to drink the "cup of sacrifice" before he could partake of the "cup of joy."

The "cup" Christ first drank from was a bitter one. In Mark 14:36, we read how Christ felt as he contemplated the covenant which was required for him to redeem his bride:

> *And he said Abba, Father, all things are possible unto thee; take away this cup from me: nevertheless, not what I will, but what thou wilt.*

Thankfully for us, Christ submitted His will to the Father and agreed to drink from the "cup of sacrifice." Even though his own disciples tried to prevent it and protect him, he was steadfast in his covenantal commitment:

> *Then said Jesus unto Peter, Put up thy sword into the sheath: the cup which my Father hath given me, shall I not drink it?* (John 18:11)

That "cup of sacrifice" would become, for all, a "cup of salvation" (or "redemption"). But at what a cost!

> *For behold, I, God, have suffered these things for all, that they might not suffer if they would repent. But if they would not repent they must suffer even as I; which suffering caused myself, even God, the greatest of all, to tremble because of pain, and to bleed at every pore, and to suffer both body and spirit—and would that I might not drink the bitter cup and shrink—nevertheless, glory be to the Father, and I partook and finished my preparations unto the children of men* (Doctrine and Covenants 19:16-19).

Because of the faithfulness of Christ, the "cup of suffering" was drunk, even to its most bitter dregs. In a wonderful way, it was then transformed into a "cup of joy" for him and his "bride."

After his resurrection, the Savior visited some of his "other sheep." He taught, blessed, and prayed for them. The feelings experienced at that time were a foreshadowing of "the cup of joy" they would share at the Great and Last Wedding Feast:

> *And after this manner do they bear record: the eye hath never seen, neither hath the ear heard, before, so great and marvelous things as we saw and heard Jesus speak unto the Father; and no tongue can speak, neither can there be written by any man, neither can the hearts of men conceive so great and marvelous things as we both saw and heard Jesus speak; and no one can conceive of the joy which filled our souls at the time we heard him pray for us unto the Father. And it came to pass that when Jesus had made an end to praying unto the Father, he arose; but so great was the joy of the multitude that they were overcome* (3 Nephi 17:16-18).

Jesus was greatly touched also—to the point of great joy:

> *...and he said unto them: Blessed are ye because of your faith. And now behold, my joy is full* (3 Nephi 17:20).

5. Bridal Chamber—Consummation

In the bridal chamber, the new couple would come to "know" one another. In Hebrew, the word "to know" is *"yada"*—meaning to have intimate experience with. This sense is used in Genesis 4:1 where Adam "knew" Eve and also in Luke 1:34 where Mary told the angel Gabriel that she did not yet "know" any man.

Another sense of the phrase "to know" was used in political treaties meaning that one acknowledged only the power and authority of their own covenantal ruler. This idea had marital application also. The vassal was to "know" (i.e. recognize) only one suzerain. (For a helpful analysis of Israel and marriage as compared to ancient suzerain-vassal treaties, see *Sinai and Zion*, Jon D. Levenson).

The Lord calls us to a relationship with Him that is close and intimate. He longs to share with us his thoughts and feelings, his joy and pain. He is deeply sensitive and willing to be vulnerable and he asks the same of us in our relationship with him and others. From such vulnerable intimacy comes knowledge, unity, and comfort. He longs to be one with us.

In the original Hebrew, the word for "one" was "*echad*," which meant a composite oneness rather than the absolute number "one." It was the word, for example, that would be used for a single cluster of grapes. It often took at least *two* to make *one*. The scriptures have many examples.

- Husband plus wife equals "one" Genesis 2:24
- Christ and the Father equals "one" John 10:30
- Christ and his disciples equals "one" John 17:20-23

This same word, *echad*, appears in Genesis 2:24 to signify that Adam and Eve became "one flesh." It appears again in Ezekiel 37:16-19 to describe the sign of the two sticks that became "one" in the prophet's hand. Zion is described as a group of individuals with "one heart and one mind" (Moses 7:18). The collective "one" of Zion was *taken* by God *unto Himself*. This terminology is obviously related to marital language. The purpose of marriage in Biblical understanding was to "become one," so that together they could "bring forth."

In the marriage chamber, the bride and groom were alone. When she removed her veil in his presence, they could then see and be seen as they really were. The need to be honestly and completely known and still accepted and loved is one of our strongest emotional needs.

David was one who was not afraid or ashamed to "stand naked" in front of the Lord. This concept has reference to more than the marriage bed; it means that we must be completely open and honest in all of our thoughts and feelings and not be afraid to share them with God. Psalm 139:1-4, 23-24 (NIV) says:

> O LORD, *you have searched me and* you know me,
> *You know when I sit and when I rise;*

> *You perceive my thoughts from afar.*
> *You discern my going out and my lying down;*
> *You are familiar with all my ways.*
> *Before a word is on my tongue you know it completely,*
>   *O LORD.*
> *Search me, O God, and know my heart;*
> *Test me and know my anxious thoughts.*
> *See if there is any offensive way in me,*
> *And lead me in the way everlasting.*

Every bride longs to completely *know* her Bridegroom. In New Testament Greek, "to know" also means "to feel." It goes beyond mere intellectual knowledge and reaches into our *hearts*. We are blessed indeed when we come to know him through our faithfulness. That is the only way we can become one with Him.

> *And I will establish my covenant with thee, and thou shalt know that I am the LORD* (Ezekiel 16:62).

If we are not faithful to our covenant promises and do not keep his commandments, we are in a state of sin, and estranged from our Beloved. John wrote about this:

> *The way we can be sure we know him is if we are obeying his commands. Anyone who says, "I know him," but doesn't obey his commands is a liar. But if someone does what he says, then truly love for God has been brought to its goal in Him. This is how we are sure that we are united with him. A person who claims to be continuing in union with him ought to conduct his life the way he did* (1 John 2:3-6 JNT).

To "know Christ" means to have intimate spiritual experience with him. And when we willingly and lovingly strive to keep his commandments, he will reveal himself to us. We know what is required to have the relationship of "knowing Christ" because of the gift of scripture that we enjoy:

> Verily thus saith the Lord, it shall come to pass that every soul who forsaketh his sins and cometh unto me, and calleth on my name, and obeyeth my voice, and keepeth my commandments shall see my face and know that I am (Doctrine and Covenants 93:1).

> And again, verily I say unto you that it is your privilege and a promise that I give unto you...that inasmuch as you strip yourselves from jealousies and fears, and humble yourself before me,...the veil shall be rent and you shall see me and know that I am—not with the carnal neither natural mind, but with the spiritual (Doctrine and Covenants 67:10).

The removal or rending of a veil gave one more intimate access. The bride in ancient days wore a veil over her hair, but today we sometimes have other veils that keep us from perceiving and knowing Christ.

> Behold, when ye shall rend the veil of unbelief which doth cause you to remain in your awful state of wickedness, and hardness of heart, and blindness of mind, then shall the great and marvelous things which have been hid up from the foundation of the world from you—when ye shall call upon the Father in my name, with a broken heart and a contrite spirit, then you shall know that the Father hath remembered the covenant which he made unto your fathers, O house of Israel (Ether 4:15).

We have an account of yet another veil that was rent:

> Jesus, when he had cried again with a loud voice, yielded up the ghost. And behold, the veil of the temple was rent in twain from the top to the bottom, and the earth did quake and the rocks rent (Matthew 27:50-51).

The veil in the temple was sixty feet wide and thirty feet tall. The thickness of the veil was one hand breadth or 3.65 inches thick. It was woven on seventy-two strands, and over each strand were twenty-two threads. The Talmud says that eighty-two young virgins were employed to make the veil. And although the veil was made under the strictest conditions of ritual purity, it nevertheless required immersion upon completion before it could be used (Shekalim 8,5). Exodus 28:32 tells about how it was prepared to be hung at the temple.

> *And there shall be an hole in the top of it, in the midst thereof: it shall have a binding of woven work round the hole of it, as it were the hole of an habergeon, that it be not rent.*

The veil was *rent*, scriptures tell us, from top to bottom. One author points out some more helpful insights.

> There could be no doubt that it was the work of God and not of men. No human hand could have done it. Rabbinic writings said that the veil was so firmly woven that two teams of oxen pulling in opposite directions, with the veil between them, could not tear it apart. The oral tradition also tells us that the priests tried to mend and sew the veil together again, but were unable to, for no thread, no cord would hold in the repaired part. It was rent once for all, and forever.
>
> Some have seen in this type that the body of the Lord Jesus Christ was represented by this veil which hung in the tabernacle between the Holy place and the Holy of Holies. Until Jesus had made the sacrifice in bearing in his own body our sins upon the tree, the way was completely barred for us to come. However, through the death of Christ, the rending of his body, and the atonement for our sins, the way to God was opened (DeHaan 115, 177).

This insight helps us to better understand what the author of Hebrews was referring to:

> *Having therefore, brethren, boldness to enter into the holiest (place) by the blood of Jesus, by a new and living*

way, which he hath consecrated for us, through the veil, that is to say, his flesh (Hebrews 10:19-20).

As a side note, there is an additional association with "rending" or "tearing" that gives us a tender insight into the sorrow Heavenly Father felt at the death of his Son. One Hebrew translation of Matthew 27:51 says, "...the curtain of the temple was *torn in two* from top to bottom."

In this one act, Heavenly Father did a very Jewish thing, but because Judaism has been downplayed in Christian understanding throughout the centuries, one can easily miss the significance of this event. In addition to the spiritual meaning spoken of in the ninth and tenth chapters of Hebrews, there is another literal understanding that is also valid. Avi Ben Mordechai sheds more light on this subject.

"I will let the ancient scribe of Second Samuel tell you its literal meaning:

While they were on their way, the report [rumor] came to David: "Absalom has struck down all the King's sons; not one of them is left." The King stood up, tore his clothes, *and lay down on the ground; and all his servants stood by with their clothes torn* (2 Samuel 13:30-31).

Here, at the death of Y'shua, is a classic example of divine Hebraic mourning. The Temple was the house of God. The *parokhet* or curtain (the partition separating the Holy of Holies from the Holy Place) was traditionally referred to as the "hem of His garment." The curtain ripping would have been understood by the priests as symbolic of God rending His garment. Remember there were tens of thousands of Jews gathered for *Pesach* (Passover) and Unleavened Bread. When news of the ripped *parokhet* passed from the priests to the people, I think it became a testimony to them. No doubt, many understood at that point Y'shua was Israel's Anointed One and that [God] was grieving over the death of His Son (Mordechai 297)."

Leaving the wedding canopy, the bride and groom retired to the marriage chamber to complete the nuptial rite. Waiting outside at the door, protecting the privacy of the bridal pair was the "friend of the bridegroom." He waited for the announcement of consummation and then received the garment or sheet that had on it the token of virginity.

Of course, if the bride was not found to be a virgin, there would be no bridegroom's shout of triumph and approval, no feasting, no celebration. One author put it this way:

> We apprehend with a crash the thought that we are the bride, and that we gave ourselves to the world long before we knew him. What will happen when he takes us to himself and unveils us, and knows that we have not been completely faithful to Him as we waited?
> "Christ loved the church," Ephesians 5 tells us, "and gave himself up for her, that he might sanctify and cleanse her—that she might be holy and blameless."
> Holy. Blameless.
> How can this be? What, we urgently ask, of the garments and the bed clothes that will not be stained? Oh, they'll be stained—not with the blood of the bride, but with the blood of our loving Groom. If we come unto Him, repentant and faithful, his blood will cover for eternity this and every other infidelity that we have ever committed (adapted Greenwood 78).

Christ will forever be the faithful witness that he loved us and washed us from our sins in his own blood.

> *Listen to him who is the advocate with the Father, who is pleading your cause before him—saying, Father, behold the sufferings and death of him who did no sin, in whom thou wast well pleased; behold the blood of thy Son which was shed....Wherefore, Father, spare these my brethren that they may come unto me and have everlasting life* (D&C 45:3-5).

6. The Wedding Feast

It is significant that the very first miracle Christ performed was at a wedding feast in Cana of Galilee, where he turned water into wine. The Lord had just returned from the extraordinary experiences of his retreat in the wilderness. Doubtless, his mind was filled with the thoughts of his work as the fulfillment of prophecy. This village wedding must have brought to him very keenly the consideration of himself as the expected Bridegroom of Israel. When his mother brought to him the troubles of the little household, "They have no wine" perhaps he was reminded of the unprepared condition of the Jews (Chavasse 58).

According to Lamsa, when Christ answered his mother, "Well, what is that to me? My hour is not yet come", Jesus was referring to the common custom of having important guests take their turn supplying the courses of wine for the feast. This was done in order. Everyone knew their assignment. If someone did it out of order, they offended the person whose turn it was. But apparently after finding that there was *no one else* who could provide the wine, he did what was necessary for the happiness of the guests and the joy of the festivities (Gospel Light 317).

It is important to remember that there were six stone jars that Christ used for his first miracle at the wedding in Cana. Every home had stone jars along with their regular pottery. Stone jars were not subject to ritual defilement so they could be used for religious washings. The water in these jars was called the "waters of purification." These stone vessels could be symbolic of the initially hard hearts of men, and the water with which they were filled would be a beautiful representation of the cleansing power of the Spirit and baptism. And since six, in Jewish understanding, is the number of man, an association could be made. Christ changed this water, which was good and pure, into wine–the symbol of his blood which was shed for us. It was also the ancient symbol for gladness and happiness. When we come to him, having made the effort to purify ourselves, we are then prepared to rejoice in the Lord.

There is another consideration. "Mine hour is not yet come" could also be a cryptic allusion to his final sufferings. The stone water pots at the marriage brought forth both water and wine. Wine was used to represent the blood of Jesus during the Passover or Last Supper the night before he died:

> *And he took the cup, and gave thanks, and gave it to them, saying, Drink ye all of it; for this is my blood of the new Testament (Covenant), which is shed for many for the remission of sins* (Matthew 26:27-28).

On the cross, the holy vessel of Jesus' body brought forth blood and water when it was pierced by the Roman soldier.

> *But one of the soldiers with a sword pierced his side, and forthwith there came out* blood *and* water (John 19:34).

Jesus began his work with the miracle at Cana to foreshadow the end of His mortal ministry on Earth. The first truly pointed to the last. In 1 John 5:6-8 we read that the blood, the water, and the Spirit all testify that Jesus was and is the Messiah:

> *And there are three that bear witness in earth, the Spirit, and the water, and the blood: and these three agree in one.*

But the cross was not the end. He has promised to give all who thirst "water from the fountain of life freely" (Revelation 21:6) and also said that at the final Wedding Feast he would again drink a "cup of joy" (Mark 14:25). Many are called and given an invitation to that great celebration. Our Heavenly Host desires that every one of His children be invited; therefore let us share with others our witness of the Beloved Bridegroom and add our own voices to this entreaty:

> *And the Spirit and the bride say, Come* (Revelation 22:17).

CHAPTER TWELVE

The Imperative of Fruitfulness

The wedding week was joyous. There were no cares for the new couple. Their accommodations were beautiful and every need and want was anticipated and bountifully met. Neither the bride nor the groom had to work or labor during this period, and their time was spent enjoying their new relationship. In many ways, the bridal chamber and the wedding week represented an Eden-like existence—whose ending would also be a new beginning.

Too soon, it seemed, the time came for both to reenter the "real world"—a world that was often filled with loneliness, dreariness, and hardship. Surely, their happiness together could continue, and even deepen, but their happiness would be ever tinged with the sorrow of being commanded to "bring forth" in a world still under a curse. The path to joy in this sphere has ever been bitter sweet.

Scholar Raphael Patai observed that the entire Hebrew world view was "saturated with the imperative of fruitfulness". The Jews believed that of the 613 commandments given to man, the very first was to "multiply and replenish the earth." It would take the man and the woman working together to accomplish God's purposes. It was vital that each stay committed and united to the other, for alone they would be unable to keep this first commandment. Together, they could grow into better individuals—enhanced in their physical, mental, and spiritual capacities. In the Lord's eyes, neither the man nor the woman were independent of each other (1 Corinthians 11:11).

Through their struggles together in the world, they would learn the real meaning behind the cups that they had shared under the marriage canopy. The "cup of sacrifice" would typify what was required so that they could share the cups of "salvation and joy."

A respected Middle Eastern Studies scholar, Carol Myers, has outlined the shared toil and responsibilities of the man and the woman in their joint effort to keep this commandment:

> God proclaims that males shall, with much hard work and unending "toil" (Gen. 3:17) struggle to produce bread (sustenance) from reluctant soils (ground that has been cursed). At the same time, the lot of females is laid out in a verse that is virtually always mistranslated and typically read through the interpretive lenses of Augustine, Milton, and many other post-Biblical commentators. Genesis 3:16 in fact sets forth the notion that God will increase both the female's "toil" (same word as in 3:17; *not* the Hebrew word for pain) and the number of her "pregnancies" (not "childbirth" as in many translations); women will have to work hard and bear many children. The text reads: I will greatly increase your toil and pregnancies; [along] with travail shall you beget children [Myers' translation 29].

We read in Genesis 3:17 that Adam was told that the ground would be cursed, but that it was to be "cursed for thy sake." Surely the intent was that all hard labor would eventuate in a blessing. Generally the consequences that Adam and Eve experienced have been interpreted only as a "punishment." But in a way otherwise not possible, this assignment of "laboring to bring forth" taught them (and us!) something about what it would cost the "Second Adam," Jesus Christ (1 Corin. 15:45-47), to "bring forth" the blessing of eternal life.

There is an interesting parallel to the idea that the land was cursed and that Adam would have to labor with difficulty to cause it to bring forth. A woman likewise was sometimes compared to "land." Frequently, in Middle Eastern terms, she was endearingly referred to as a "garden." The analogy is obvious. Just as a garden receives seed and brings forth, so does a woman. It is worth noting that another term for "gardener" is "husbandman."

A scripture that correlates *land* with *wife* is found in Jeremiah 3:1:

> *They say, If a man put away his wife and she go from him, and become another man's, shall he return to her again? Shall not that* land *be greatly polluted? but thou hast played the harlot with many lovers; yet return again to me saith the LORD.*

In this verse, *wife* is in parallel with *land*. Parallelisms in Hebrew writings often indicate similar ideas and meanings. There is another associated parallel and numeric link between land, woman, and honey. The Hebrew word for *honey–De VaSh* –has the numerical value of 306. The Hebrew word for *woman– IshaH*–also equals 306. A woman–like the *land* of Israel–is a source of milk and honey (Blech 154). She is meant to be a blessing, and her body is a symbol representing the Abrahamic blessings of an eternal posterity and land of inheritance forever.

Adam was required to toil to bring forth from the land. Along with Adam, both "lands"–the earth and the woman–were under the same curse. Essentially the curse was that in order to have the blessing of fruitfulness and fertility–much labor was required. It took travail to bring forth. Since fertility was *always* considered a blessing, the difficulties associated with the process of bringing forth were considered well worth the price. Great effort was required of both the man and the woman.

> *And it came to pass, that after I, the Lord God, had driven them out, that Adam began to till the earth, and to have dominion over all the beasts of the field, and to eat his bread by the sweat of his brow, as I, the Lord had commanded him, and Eve also, his wife, did labor with him* (Genesis 4:1 JST).

There was a division of labor from the beginning, though certainly there was much overlap. The woman's unique capacity and primary responsibility was to give birth and care for the couple's children. Since her "land" (her body) was mortal, this assignment required labor and travail. After each birth, her labor continued through giving needed nourishment and care to their offspring.

The man bore the heavy responsibility of sustaining his family. Not only was he required to labor on the land to bring forth from fields, trees, and vineyards, he often had to care also for flocks and herds of animals. The work of his hands produced everything needful including *bread, oil, wine,* and *meat.* Surprisingly, although meal preparation and serving were traditionally "women's work", the scriptures, with very few exceptions, have men "bringing forth" the four symbolic foods mentioned above. And in one exception (Ruth 2:18) a woman was acting in the traditional masculine role of provider. Clearly, there is some association between these elements of sacral meals, a man's labors, and his assignment to "bring forth" bread and wine for covenant establishment and renewal.

> *And Melchizedek king of Salem* brought forth *bread and wine: and he was the priest of the most high God* (Genesis 14:18).

The Savior's actions when feeding the five thousand were consistent with the principle of having men—not the women—"bring forth" (or "set before") the foods associated with covenantal meals. Just as the mother must constantly provide both nourishment and physical care for her children, these scriptures seem to indicate that the father, likewise, is to provide spiritual sustenance as well as physical support.

Additionally, just as a woman gave birth, a man, through his assignment to labor and teach others about the Gospel brought God's children to a *new birth* and spiritual creation through baptism. When a lack of true teachers caused a "famine of hearing the words of the Lord (Amos 8:11)," preaching the Gospel caused the famine to cease and the earth to be "replenished" spiritually (Genesis 1:28 & 9:1).

150 / THE IMPERATIVE OF FRUITFULNESS

An abbreviated summary of the processes of childbirth, toiling to bring forth "bread" (food), and missionary labor shows some remarkable similarities.

Giving Birth	Agricultural Toil	Missionary Labor
Requires 2 to become 1	Requires 2 elements -- man and fertile soil	Requires 2 -- teacher and learner
Requires a fertile seed to be planted	Requires a good seed and place for planting	Requires good seed (truth) planted through preaching
Womb is prepared to nurture seed	Ground must be prepared to nurture seed	Heart prepared to receive "seed"
Seed is nourished during development	Garden must be tended and watered	Seed must be nourished (Alma 32:37)
Time is required for development	Time is required for the plants to grow	Time is required to develop a testimony
"Heaviness" as child develops	Heads of wheat are heavy-- bowed down	The heaviness of sin is a burden (Jacob 2:9)
Labor required to bring forth *tazria* -- literally "bring forth seed"	Requires much labor to harvest	Labor required to bring to baptism
Child brought forth in sorrow from water & blood	Seed "sown in tears" sweat & blood bring forth	Sorrowing over sins New life through waters of baptism & blood of the atonement
After travail comes great joy	Great joy and rejoicing in the harvest	Teacher has great joy in the fruit of his labors (Alma 36:25)
Child tenderly protected and nourished	Grain carefully protected and stored	New member tenderly nourished with "milk" of word
Child grows to maturity and can become a parent	Harvested grain can be used as seed to begin the cycle anew	The learner can progress to spiritual maturity and become a teacher to others

There is another association between these three life-givers. In ancient Israel whenever a temple existed, the Law of Moses required that a portion of all "first fruits" be brought there as an offering in token of the whole. The understanding was that when God accepted a part, He also sanctified the whole.

- First fruit of the womb—the firstborn son—brought to the temple.
- First fruits of earth—seven species—brought to the temple.
- Fruits of missionary labors—the proselytes—were brought to the temple.

This next section will focus on the double aspects of birth and rebirth, with their associated physical organs. According to scriptural teachings, this dual process of life-giving was a source of salvation for both the man and his wife. 1 Timothy 2:15 states:

> *Notwithstanding,* they *shall be* saved *in* childbearing, *if they continue in faith and charity and holiness with sobriety* (JST).

The Doctrine and Covenants compares their joint capacity to bear fruit to a tree:

> *For I the Lord will cause* them *to bring forth as a very fruitful tree which is planted in a goodly land, by a pure stream that yieldeth much precious fruit* (D&C 97:9).

Trees were commonly compared to people in Hebrew thought. A *willingness to bear* was an important element of salvation. Luke 13:9 states:

> *And if it* bear fruit, *the tree is* saved, *and if not, after that thou shalt cut it down* (JST).

The purpose of marriage in Hebrew understanding was to *bear fruit.* There are many ways to do so. Besides childbirth, some of them are:

- *Fruit* in terms of souls   Proverbs 11:30
- *Fruits* meet for repentance   Matthew 3:8

152 / THE IMPERATIVE OF FRUITFULNESS

- *Fruits* of the Spirit   Galatians 5:22
- *Fruits* of our lips (praise)   Hebrews 13:15

Good fruit was borne not only by "trees" but also through "chosen vessels." There were several kinds of vessels made by ancient potters. When we learn more about what these vessels represented in the context of Middle Eastern pottery making, we can gain a fuller understanding of their symbolism. In Romans 9:21-23 we read:

> Hath not the potter power over the clay, of the same lump to make one vessel unto honor and another unto dishonor [i.e. for common use]? What if God...endured with much long-suffering the vessels of wrath *fitted to destruction*...that he might make known the riches of his glory on the vessels of mercy...

For purposes of this chapter concerning the ideas of bringing forth and bearing, representative examples of a vessel of wrath, a vessel of mercy, and a chosen vessel will be used. There are many types of vessels mentioned in scripture. For example: a vessel of honor (2 Timothy 2:20-21), a vessel "empty of pleasure" (Jeremiah 22:28), an abominable vessel (Isaiah 65:4), a clean vessel (Isaiah 66:20), and a holy vessel (Isaiah 52:11). To follow up on more than just a few of these vessels as types would take us too far afield from the subject at hand. (Barbara M. Bowen addresses this topic at some length in her book, *Strange Scriptures that Perplex the Western Mind.*)

Vessels of Wrath and Vessels of Mercy

Piles of broken vessels were frequently found on the floor of ancient pottery shops. These were called *vessels of wrath* and were useless to the potter. They appeared absolutely all right until they were put into the furnace. They came out cracked because they could not take the heat. The potter was unwilling to just cast them aside, so he would attempt to repair them. The potter prepared a certain kind of cement out of blood from a small insect called the *fasuka* which lived on the body of a bull. The potter took the blood of the *fasuka* and mixed it with some powdered broken pottery and cemented the crack in his vessel. He would put more wet clay on it, reheat it, refire it, and if it held the patch, it was called a *vessel of mercy*. (A vessel of mercy was used to carry fresh water which was freely shared.) Sometimes the first repair attempt would be unsuccessful. Then the potter would patiently seek to repair the vessel several times; but if it would not hold his "mercy" patch, it would become a *vessel of wrath*. He would finally break it and use the pieces for some other purpose.

Chosen Vessels

These vessels typified trust, reliability, and faithfulness. Travelers were often desirous to take home a representative vessel showing the workmanship of the craftsmen in that area. One could request that the potter choose the very best from among all his vessels. After selecting the vessel the potter would hand it to the traveler saying, "I will never be ashamed to send this vessel to any part of the world, for I have chosen it, and I know it will never put me to shame. It is a *chosen vessel*. It may look the same to you as the other vessels; it may not even seem very attractive, but it will stand the test. Because it will bring me honor, I have *chosen* this *vessel* (See Ephesians 1:4) (Bowen 118)."

Both men and women were designated as *chosen vessels*. Mary was named in scripture as having this title of honor:

> And behold, he shall be born of Mary...she being a virgin, *a precious and* chosen vessel, *who shall be over-shadowed and conceive by the power of the Holy Ghost; and* bring forth *a son, yea, even the son of God* (Alma 7:10).

Paul the Apostle was also identified with the same phrase in Acts 9:15:

> But the Lord said unto him (Ananias), Go thy way: for he (Paul) is a chosen vessel unto me, to bear my name before the Gentiles, and kings, and the children of Israel.

Mary *brought forth* the *son* of God, also known as *the Word* (John 1:1). Paul was called to *bear* the message, *the word of God,* to the world. It seems apparent that men and women have virtually the same assignment—to bring life and light into the world—they just use different means. This can be illustrated in a parallel statement.

Mary // a chosen vessel // brought forth // the Son of God // (The Word).
Paul // a chosen vessel // bore // the message // (The word of God).

Both of them sought to *glorify* God by their actions. In Jewish understanding, *glory* was always associated with the *ability to give life* and indicated also a willingness to labor and suffer affliction in order to bring forth. Work and glory were inseparably connected. The root word in Hebrew (Strong 3513) identifies glory with weightiness—the glory from life-giving carried a heavy weight of responsibility (D&C 63:66). Hosea 9:11 tells of a devastating time in Israel's history when Ephraim was shorn of his *glory* or ability to give life:

> *Ephraim's* glory *will fly away like a bird—no birth, no pregnancy, no conception* (NIV).

A woman was an important source of glory to her husband (1 Corinthians 11:7). Without her, he had no capacity to give life. The Biblical perspective was: no wife = little glory. Whenever a husband and wife gave life or when a mentor helped another experience the process of spiritual rebirth, the Lord was glorified.

The glory of the Lord also rested upon his temples because they were holy. According to Jewish understanding, *life* (and potential life) is *holy*. *Blood* was also considered *holy* because it represented *life*. In the ancient temple, *sacrifices* and *blood* were associated together because of the *holiness* of the *life* that was given to provide the sacrifice. No greater sacrifice could be offered. The animal sacrifices were seen as a type that man must put off his animal-like urges (worldly and natural) which kept his spiritual nature from being strengthened (Mosiah 3:19). The Law of Sacrifice was the means given whereby man's moral and spiritual life could be restored and purified. In Jewish thought, the laws of sacrifice were associated with God's attributes of divine love and mercy. The experience of bringing a sacrifice enabled each person to vicariously experience death and to understand what was required to overcome sin. The sacrifices were not an end in themselves. The sin offering was not acceptable unless it was accompanied by true repentance (Richman 9). The Jews taught that it would be preferable that man *not* sin, and then no offering would be necessary (Babylonian Talmud, Berakhot 22:A); but all had sinned, therefore sacrifice was required.

The most sacred of all sacrifices was offered once a year in the Jewish Temple on *Yom Kippur*. After ten days involving fasting and repentance, the nation of Israel, sought to be reconciled or made at-one with their God. *Blood* was offered in the *Holy of Holies* by the High Priest as an atonement that, worthily offered, brought spiritual *life* for all of the people. *Life* and *blood* were always associated with the highest *holiness* in the holiest place—the temple.

The temple was also compared to the physical body. In Paul's letter to the Corinthians, he teaches this principle:

> Know ye not that ye are the temple of God, and that the spirit of God dwelleth in you? If any man defile the temple of God, him shall God destroy; for the temple of God is holy, which temple ye are (1 Cor. 3:16-17).

The scripture above reminds us that the highest holiness was associated with the temple, and much of that holiness was related to the sacrifices given there.

Throughout history, men have been required in times of war to give their lives and shed their heart's blood in defense of their lands, religious freedom, and the lives of their wives and children. They also made many sacrifices to provide for their families.

Women must also shed their blood to give life. Indeed, the very capacity to give life *requires* the ability to shed blood and is impossible without this capability. The women likewise sacrifice so that the needs of their families can be met.

Life-giving capacity is especially associated with two organs in the body, the heart and the womb. These two organs appear to serve as types for the holiest of holy places in one's own bodily temple. They are *holy* precisely because they are the means of giving *life* - physical and spiritual.

Just as the womb is associated with birth, so is the heart vital for spiritual *re*birth. There are many physical and spiritual similarities between the two organs.

- Both are sacred and should be guarded carefully. Life issues from both (Pro. 4:23).
- Both are associated with the flow of blood (life).
- Both are pear shaped.
- Both receive "seed" in the heart, the word can be compared to a seed. (Alma 32)
- Both have the power to conceive. (Luke 1:31 and Acts 5:4)
- Both enlarge or "swell" when conception takes place. (Alma 32:28)
- Both organs hang by ligaments in a body cavity.
- Both are extremely strong muscles with great power to bring forth.
- The heart requires blood for nourishment and the baby in the womb is nourished by the blood of the placenta.
- The muscles of both organs contract regularly
- The contractions prepare the womb for the exertion of birth. Strong contractions caused by exercise also

strengthen the heart.
- The child in the womb is surrounded by a membrane sac containing watery fluid–the amniotic sac. In scriptural terms, this membrane is known as a "caul". The heart is also surrounded by a membrane sac containing a small amount of watery fluid–the pericardial sac. This membrane is mentioned as a "caul" in Hosea 13:8.
- For both the heart and the womb, the preparations to "bring forth" are time consuming and frequently cause discomfort due to stretching.

Just as a baby develops in the womb, a testimony develops in the heart. For both a baby and a spiritual witness, a means to deliver a "seed" and a way to "bear fruit" are required. Not surprisingly, the body has two parts that are remarkably similar in function and appearance. These two parts are the larynx and the cervix. Medical anatomy books contain pictures of each that show startling similarities.

Larynx	Cervix
Opening to a passage in the throat	Opening to a passage in the "neck"
Associated membrane covering	Associated membrane covering
Bound with ligaments	Bound with ligaments
Vocal "folds" that open and close	Folds that open and close
Brings forth fruit of the heart	Brings forth fruit of the womb

Tissues from every single body part have distinctive characteristics and can be readily identified with their respective organs. However, the cervix and larynx are the only two parts of the body with identical cell tissue. Although there are variances during the monthly cycle, at any given time identical color and mucus count will be found in both. Samples taken from the larynx and cervix are indistinguishable from each other even under a microscope (Joseph 32).

The physical similarities between these two body parts seem to indicate a correlation between giving birth to children and giving life to our words. Speaking is much like giving birth. Air pressure (from a contracting diaphragm) propels the voice past the vocal folds of the throat into the world. And in a process remarkably similar, a child is expelled into the world. Just as excess tension impedes the delivery of a baby, fear tightens the throat and vocal constrictions make it difficult or impossible to deliver a message. A message is composed of words. In Hebrew "words," *devarim*, also means "things." Words were thought to be extremely powerful–a tangible creation.

When we understand the relationship between birthing and speaking, and that both introduce "life" into the world, little wonder then that the Lord holds us strictly accountable for what we "bring forth" out of our hearts. Just as each parent must give a report regarding his or her stewardship with each child, so is every individual held accountable for the words he speaks and for the influence those words have.

Matthew 12:36 teaches the principle:

> *But I say unto you, That every idle word that men shall speak, they shall give account thereof in the day of judgment.*

We follow Christ's example and bless others when we are willing to use our words to bear witness of the Savior.

> *To this end was I born, and for this cause came I into the world, that I should bear witness to the truth* (John 18:37).

Words of testimony are to the hearts of those who hear as the warmth and light of the sun is to the earth. Each provides a crucial element for growth. A refusal to share light–life–when we have it does not please the Lord:

> *But with some I am not well pleased, for they will not open their mouths, but they hide the talent which I have given unto them, because of the fear of man* (D&C 60:2).

The pattern regarding life-giving in scripture, although traditionally a feminine concept, applies to both the man and the woman. Sometimes there are difficulties with scriptural imagery because of gender. The predominantly masculine terminology and patriarchal emphasis of the scriptures has estranged some women. Likewise, men sometimes find themselves uncomfortable with the feminine nature of bridal symbolism and childbirth imagery. Each are unsure about how to "liken it unto themselves."

What we have in scripture is a patriarchal history replete with feminine imagery. Just as it took two—man and woman—to be called "Adam" (Genesis 5:2), the scriptures needed both elements to be complete. Their words show everyone how to become like Christ. Of course, this does not mean to assume a masculine role, but to imitate His good qualities. The traits and virtues that Christ exemplifies have both masculine and feminine associations. For example, justice is typically thought of as masculine, while mercy has a feminine correlation.

> *For behold, justice exerciseth all his demands, and also mercy claimeth all which is her own...* (Alma 42:24)

Christ is perfect in both qualities. He is able to unify seemingly contradictory attributes and model the best of both in appropriate contexts.

During mortality, Jesus was a fierce defender of the sanctity of his Father's house and was severe against all corruption. Yet he was also perfectly submissive to the will of his Father and was kind and tender with the little ones who were brought to him. The first time he came as the Suffering Servant but, when he comes again, He has promised that it will be as the triumphant Warrior-King who returns to take his bride with power and great glory.

Christ's "bride" in scripture is his Church, and, of course, the Church is composed of both males and females who become "*one* heart and *one* mind." He loves his "bride" with undistracted devotion. So too, our commitment to our Beloved Bridegroom—Jesus Christ—will automatically preclude relationships with other people or philosophies that would draw us away from Him. If we desire to be "chosen," we must strive continually to be found worthy and focus solely on pleasing Him. Any other course will disqualify us to be His bride. There are only two kinds of brides—one who is virtuous and faithful in keeping covenants and one who is in any way unfaithful and chooses to remain impure in body or thought.

There are many examples of faithful brides in scripture whose experiences foreshadow Christ and show how he relates to his "bride." Ada Habershon lists some of them in her book, *Types in the Old Testament*. A sampling follows:

> *Eve* was given to Adam and she was to become "one" with him. This is the same goal that Christ has for his church, that we become one with each other and with him. Additional scriptures relating to this are John 17:6 and John 17:21, 23.
>
> *Rebekah* was another bride who was fetched from her home, just as a bride was taken from her home to the house of her bridegroom. It was taught that Abraham had given Isaac "all that he hath." Christ also received all that *His* Father hath; and Christ is willing to bestow the same upon us as we accept Him for our bridegroom. Scriptures concerning this are found in Genesis 24:4-8 and John 17:6-16. Isaac prayed for Rebekah as she journeyed. In John 17:9 & 15, we're told that Christ prayed for us, His bride—His people.
>
> *Rachel* was won by long service. Christ also served and paid a price for us (Genesis 29:20).
>
> *Ruth* became a bride by Boaz's acceptance of the

responsibility to redeem her (Ruth 3:18 and Ruth 4:14). Although a gentile by birth, she sought for his "covering" (another word for Atonement) and found love and safety with him. For each one who seeks his sheltering cover, Christ provides "rest." Recall that in Hebrew, one meaning of "rest" is "security in the house of a husband."

Michal was the bride of David and she was given to him as a reward for his victory over the Philistines (1 Samuel 17:25 and John 17:4). Christ's bride, his church, is given to him as a reward for his victory over death.

Sarah was the bride of Abraham. She called her husband "Lord" (1 Peter 3:6) and was under his law. Such righteous submission is reflected in Christ's submission to the law of his Father.

Zipporah was the bride of Moses and, interestingly enough, she became his bride after he had laid aside the princely glory of Egypt and had come down to where she lived in the desert. Christ also laid aside his glory from the premortal existence and came down to earth to ask us to be His bride (Exodus 2:21 and John 17:5). We are the object of his love, and his desire is to have us with him (John 17:10, 23-24).

With regard to Jesus Christ, each person can see themselves in the position of a bride: greatly loved (although generally undeserving), redeemed, comforted, and called to the joy and happiness of mutual devotion. The purpose of Biblical marriage has always been to be united in covenant and, through knowledge, bear fruit and enable new life to come forth.

Just as a pregnancy can be evident to everyone, our testimony and spiritual fruits can be obvious to others. In Acts 4:13, John and Peter were identified as unschooled ordinary men; but as the people observed their confidence and faithfulness to the Lord, they marveled. In the King James translation, the people exclaimed that these men "knew" Him, or that "they had been with Jesus." This "knowing" has the same depth as the term in Genesis 4:1 when it speaks of the intimate relations Eve had when she "knew" or "had been with" her husband (Kendall 72). John and Peter through their faith in Christ *gave* a man who had been lame from birth a *new life*—he was healed in body and filled with praise and rejoicing. The actions and words of John and Peter demonstrated an intimate association with their master, Jesus Christ.

Our reverence, loyalty, and devotion to the Bridegroom will also manifest our knowledge of Him. Others will also see that we know and love Him because of the sweet fruits we bring forth. Paul's prayer in Ephesians 3:17-21 portrays the tender relationship available to *all* who lovingly seek Him. Surely they shall find their heart's desire.

> *And I pray that Christ will be more and more at home in your hearts as you trust in him. May your roots go down deep into the soil of God's marvelous love. And may you have power to understand as all saints should, how wide, how long, how high, and how deep his love really is. May you experience the love of Christ, although it is so great you will never fully understand it. Then you will be filled with the fullness of life and power that comes from God.*
>
> *Now glory be to God! By his mighty power at work within us, he is able to accomplish infinitely more than we would ever dare to ask or hope. May he be given glory in the church and in Christ Jesus throughout all generations, for ever and ever! Amen* (NLT & NIV).

APPENDIX I

Outline

I. Kiddushin - Marriage by Law
    A. Erusin
    B. Nissu'in

II. Erusin - Betrothal
    A. Choosing - initiative
    B. Proposal - negotiation of bride price
    C. Contract - Ketuba
    D. Offering of gift
    E. Acceptance by Bride
    F. Ritual Statement & Consecration
    G. Witnesses - three elements

III. Preparation for Marriage
    A. Groom's responsibilities/friend's duties
    B. Bride - Changes and preparation

IV. Nissu'in - Wedding
    A. Father's approval - son takes bride
    B. Bride and her attendants (10 virgins)
    C. Arrival of Bridal Pair
    D. Wedding canopy
    E. Bridal Chamber - Consummation
    F. Wedding Feast
    G. New Home Established - blessed with posterity

APPENDIX II

Torah
The five Book of Moses: Genesis, Exodus, Leviticus, Numbers, Deuteronomy

Talmud
A collection of teachings that is composed of two parts:
1. *Mishnah* - a topical presentation of the oral tradition relating to the Torah with its associated rabbinic discussions. It consists of six sections divided into 63 tractates.
2. *Gemara* - commentaries on the *Mishnah*.

There are two versions of the Talmud:
1. *The Jerusalem Talmud* - which is older, smaller, and less well known.
2. *The Babylonian Talmud* - was written largely by Diaspora rabbis living in or near Babylon. Considered authoritative. (Jews taken from the land of Israel were considered part of the Diaspora.)

Midrash Rabbah
Includes discussions, homilies, and allegories that relate to the Old Testament

Tanakh
The Jews usually call the Old Testament the *Tanakh*, an acronym formed from the Hebrew names for each section:
- *Torah* - the five books of Moses ("instruction" or "law")
- *Nevi'im* - (Prophets) including: the "former prophets": Joshua, Judges, 1 and 2 Samuel, and 1 and 2 Kings;

and the "latter prophets": Isaiah, Jeremiah, Ezekiel, and the Book of the Twelve (Hosea, Joel, Amos, Obadiah, Jonah, Micah, Nahum, Habakkuk, Zephaniah, Haggai, Zechariah, and Malachi).
- *Ketuvim* - (Writings) including: the Psalms, Job, Proverbs, Ruth, Song of Solomon, Lamentations, Esther, Daniel, Ezra, Nehemiah, and 1 and 2 Chronicles.

For Jews, these three parts of the Bible do not have the same status. "Moses received the Torah on Sinai and passed it on...." This sentence from Jewish tradition expresses the fact that Judaism sees the Torah as the fundamental revelation. All further revelation and scriptural interpretation, oral or written, is related to and measured by the event on Sinai (Limburg 156).

GLOSSARY OF HEBREW TERMS

Hebrew vowels and diphthongs are pronounced like those italicized in the following words: f*a*ther, *ai*sle, b*e*d, n*ei*ghbor, *i*nvest (Usually when not accented) or mar*i*ne (Usually when accented), *o*bey, r*u*le, "ch" is pronounced as in Johann Sebastian Ba*ch*, and so is "kh"; "g" is always hard (give); other consonants are more or less as in English. Accented syllables are printed in **boldface**.

a · **bad** -- work, service, or worship
ab · **ba** -- daddy
a · **don** -- lord and master
A · do · **nai** -- my Lord, Lord of all; spoken by Jewish people instead of God's personal name Y-H-V-H ("Jehovah").
a · **per** · i · on -- a Greek term meaning bridal chair or litter
A · **ron**-ha · Ko · **desh** -- where the Torah scrolls are kept in the synagogue
a · **sar** -- to bind
b'nai-**hup** · pah -- children of the bride chamber
ba'al -- master
Baal Shem Tov -- a title of respect given to Israel ben Eliezer, a famous Rabbi (1700-1760)
bar-**mitz** · vah -- "Son of the Law" ceremony for a 13-year-old Jewish boy
be'**u** · lah -- wife
be · ma -- stand or pulpit
ber · ith -- (the "h" is silent) a covenant
bet-hat · a · **nut** -- the bridal chamber
bik · ku · **rim** -- the first fruits offerings
Bir · kat - ha · **Ma** · zon -- the Blessing after Meals
cha · **gag** -- to move in a circle
chev · lai-shel-**Ma** · **shi** · ach -- Birth pangs of the Messiah
d'**vash** -- honey or syrup from ripe dates
dam -- blood
da · **mim** -- the plural of blood, also one of the names for money in Hebrew because it represents man's labor and risks
dev · a · **rim** -- words

e · chad -- one or oneness
e · ru · sin -- betrothal ceremony including: proposal, negotiation of bride price, and the bride's acceptance
e · zar -- helper
get -- divorce
gib · or ·ei-Yis · ra · el -- the heroes of Israel
gid -- sinew
go'el --kinsman redeemer
hag or chag -- feast
hag · i · a · zo -- a Greek term meaning to dedicate or rededicate, particularly in reference to a temple
haw/hav -- the Semitic root meaning "love"
ho · reh -- parent
hok · mah -- wisdom
hup · pa -- wedding canopy
im · ma -- momma
ish · ah -- woman
je · shu-ah -- salvation
ka'lal -- to complete, to perfect, or to consummate
kab · ba · lat-pa · nim -- "meeting of the faces" greeting friends and family at a wedding
kal · lah -- a bride
ka · rat-ber · it -- to make or "cut" a covenant
ke · tho · neth -- to make a covering for
ke ·tu · ba -- a formal marriage contract
ke· tu · bot -- wedding contract (plural)
kid · du · shin -- sanctification, also a term used for marriage
kit · tel -- a white tunic or coat tied with a white sash
kor · ban-le-hak · riv -- sacrifice
le · hem -- bread
lev -- heart
ma · hal -- to forgive
ma · zel-tov -- good luck or good fortune
me'ku · de · shet -- a bride, one who is betrothed
me · lah -- salt
me · zu · za -- a ritual object placed on a door frame
mik · vah -- a ritual immersion
Mish · nah -- the oral teachings concerning the Torah
mo · har -- the bride price
ne · ge · do -- suitable or appropriate
nis · su'in -- the time between betrothal and consummation

na · su -- to carry
par · o · khet -- a veil or curtain separating the Holy of Holies from the Holy Place
Pe · sach -- Passover
ra · cham -- mercy
ra · vak -- empty, a term for a bachelor
rech · em -- womb
rim · mon -- a bell, also pomegranate
Sar-Sha · lom -- Prince of Peace
sa · vah -- to be satisfied or fulfilled, the root of *shevah* or seven
se · gu · lah -- a hidden (peculiar) treasure
Shab · bat -- the Sabbath
sha · kar -- a strong drink expressed from fruits other than the grape
sha · lom-ba · yit -- a peaceful home
shaph · ka -- an instrument for pouring out
shem tov -- a shining name
shema -- to hear, listen, or pay attention
she · va-ber · a · chot -- the seven wedding blessings
she · vah -- seven
sho · far -- a ceremonial horn also referred to as a "trumpet"
tal · lit -- a fringed prayer shawl
Tal · mud -- see Appendix II
Ta · mar -- a girl's name meaning "date palm"
tav -- the last letter of the Hebrew alphabet
te · tel · les · tai -- a Greek word meaning "it is finished" or "paid in full"
Tor · ah -- see Appendix II
ya · da -- to be intimately associated, or to know
yar · eh -- teaching or instruction
ya · yin -- juice or wine from grapes
yi · chud -- seclusion for the bride and groom
Yom-Kip · pur -- the Highest Holy Day, the Day of Atonement

INDEX

A
Accepting a name...........118
Adultery/apostasy...........120

B
Beauty...........14
Birth pangs of the Messiah...........133
Boys...........7
Bread...........72, 82
Bridegroom's gift of value...........28, 114, 115
Bride price...........21, 108
Bride veiled...........31, 126
Brides in Scripture...........159

C
Cana...........144
Charity...........52
Chart...........150
Comforter...........123
Community as corporate body...........17
Companion...........20, 128
Crowns...........103
Cup of sacrifice...........136
Cutting covenant...........18

D
Dates(honey)...........80
Dating...........11
Door-keeper...........50
Dried-up/withered...........78

E
Echad, one...........138
Eliezar...........15

F
Father, duties..5
Fat tail of sheep..84
Figs...77
Fire, metaphor for love..13
Friend of Bridegroom..120,124

G
Garment of Light..54
Girls..7,8
Glory..154
Grapes..74

H
Harvest...12
Hate, as technical term..25
Helpmeet..8
Holiness of life, sacrifice..155
Holy of Holies..62
Hosea as type...iii
Hospitality...69

I
Immersion, definition..37
Invitations to feast...40

J
JAMA article..117
Jealous, Biblical definition..63

K
Ketubah...26, 111
'Knowing' the Lord..137
Korban..37

L
Larynx/cervix...157
Light...47

M
Marriage canopy..55
Meat...83
Mercy...134
Mikvah, hope..125
Modesty..63
Mother's contribution..9

O
Old age as blessing..101
Olives..75
Outer darkness..49

P
Paid in full..110
Party manners...92
Peaceful home...105
Pomegranates...80
Prosperity..104

R
Ransom...113
Rending of veil..139

S
Sabbath, as gift and bride........................115, 127
Sabbath songs...95, 128
Salt in covenant-making....................................20
Seating...90
Seven bridal blessings..58
Shema..5
Song of Solomon...90

T
Tallit..39
Temple..9, 102
Thief in the night...130
Travail..133
Tying the knot...35

V
Vassal, Suzerain..........137
Veil of the temple..........140
Veil torn as sign of grief..........142
Vessels..........152

W
Water as a symbol..........97
Wedding ceremony..........56
Wedding garment..........51
Wedding procession..........43
Wedding song..........88
Wheat..........71
White caps..........54
White garments..........53
Witnesses..........120
Woman as "land"..........148
Womb/heart..........156

SELECTED BIBLIOGRAPHY

Aiken, Lisa. *To Be a Jewish Woman*. London: Aronson, 1992.

Alexander, David and Pat. *Eerdman's Handbook to the Bible*. England: Lion Publishing, 1983.

Ausubel, Nathan. *The Book of Jewish Knowledge*. New York: Crown Publishers, 1964.

Bailey, Albert. *Daily Life in Bible Times*. New York: Charles Scribner's Sons, 1943.

Bailey, Kenneth E. *Poet and Peasant*. Grand Rapids: Eerdmans, 1976.

— *Through Peasant Eyes*. Grand Rapids: Eerdmans, 1976.

Barclay, William. *The Daily Study Bible Series*. Philadelphia: Westminster Press, 1975.

— *The Gospel of Mark*. Philadelphia: Westminster Press, 1954.

— *Introducing the Bible*. Nashville: Abingdon Press, 1997.

— *The Mind of Jesus*. San Francisco: Harper Collins, 1960.

Barrett, C.K. Editor. *The New Testament Background*. San Francisco: Harper Collins, 1989.

Berkowitz, Ariel and D'vorah. *Torah Rediscovered*. Littleton, Colorado: First Fruits of Zion, 1996.

Bilezikian, Gilbert. *Beyond Sex Roles*. 2nd ed. Michigan: Baker Book House, 1985.

Bivin, David, and Roy Blizzard. *Understanding the Difficult Words of Jesus*. Arcadia: Makor Foundation, 1983.

Blech, Benjamin. *The Secrets of Hebrew Words*. Northvale: Jason Aronson, 1991.

Blenkinsopp, Joseph. "The Family in First Temple Israel." Browning, 48-103.

Booker, Richard. *Here Comes the Bride*. USA: Sounds of the Trumpet Inc., 1995.

Bouquet, A.C. *Everyday Life in New Testament Times*. New York: Charles Scribner's Sons, 1953.

Bowen, Barbara. *Strange Scriptures that Perplex the Western Mind*. Grand Rapids: Wm. B. Eerdman Publishing, 1940

* Browning, Don S. and Ian S. Evison. ed. *Families in Ancient Israel*. Louisville, Kentucky: Westminister John Knox Press, 1997.

* Bullinger, E.W. *Numbers in Scripture*. Grand Rapids, Michigan: Kregel Publications, 1967.

Chadwick, Harold and James Freeman. *The New Manners and Customs of the Bible*. North Brunswick, New Jersey: Bridge-Logos Publishers, 1998.

Charlesworth, James H. Editor. *Jesus' Jewishness - Exploring the Place of Jesus in Early Judaism*. New York: Crossroad Publishing Co., 1991.

Chavasse, C. *The Bride of Christ*. London: Faber and Faber, 1940.

Chill, Abraham. *The Minagim - Customs and Ceremonies of Judaism, Their Origins and Rationale*. New York: Sepher-Hermon Press, 1979.

Chilton, David. *Paradise Restored*. Texas: Reconstruction Press, 1985.

* Chumney, Edward. *The Seven Festivals of the Messiah*. Shippensburg: Destiny Image, 1994.

* Cohen, Abraham. *Everyman's Talmud*. 1940 New York: Schocken, 1996.

Coleman, William. *Today's Handbook of Bible Times and Customs*. Minneapolis, Minnesota: Bethany House Publishers, 1940.

Collins, John J. "Marriage, Divorce, and Family in Second Temple Judaism" Browning, 104-162.

Daniel-Rops, Henri. *Daily Life in the Time of Jesus*. Ann Arbor, Michigan: Servant Books, 1980.

Daube, David. *The New Testament and Rabbinic Judaism*. 1956. Reprint. Peabody, Mass.: Hendrickson, 1994.

Day, Colin. *Roget's Thesaurus of the Bible*. San Francisco:

Harper Collins, 1992.

De Boer, P.A. *Fatherhood and Motherhood in Israelite and Judean Piety.* Leiden: E.J. Brill, 1974.

DeHaan, M.R. *The Tabernacle.* Grand Rapids: Zondervan, 1955.

DeVaux, Roland. *Ancient Israel.* Translated by John McHugh. New York: McGraw - Hill Book Company, 1961.

Dockrey, K. *Holman Student Bible Dictionary.* Nashville: Holman Bible Publishers, 1993.

Drane, John. *The Life that Changed the World.* Oxford: Lion Publishing, 1994.

Drucker, Malka. *Celebrating Life - Jewish Rites of Passage.* New York: Holiday House.

Earle, Ralph. *Word Meanings in the New Testament.* Peabody, Mass.: Hendrickson Publishers, 1974.

Edersheim, Alfred. *Bible History Old Testament.* Peabody, Mass.: Hendrickson Publishers, 1995.

— *The Life and Times of Jesus the Messiah.* Grand Rapids: Eerdmans Publishing House, 1983.

— *Sketches of Jewish Social Life.* Grand Rapids: Eerdmans Publishing House, 1986.

— *The Temple In Jesus' Day.* Grand Rapids: Eerdmans Publishing House, 1986.

— *The Temple - Its Ministry and Services.* Updated Edition. Peabody, Mass.: Hendrickson, 1995.

Embry, Margaret. *Growing Up in Bible Times.* Nashville: Thomas Nelson Publishers, 1995.

Engelsman, Joan. *The Feminine Dimension of the Divine.* Wilmette, Illinois: Chiron Publications, 1987.

Errico, Rocco. *Let There Be Light.* Santa Fe, New Mexico: Noohra Foundation, 1994.

Farrar, Frederic. *The Life of Christ.* 1874. Portland, Oregon: Fountain Publications, 1980.

Flaugher, Dewey. *Behold, The Bridegroom Cometh - For His Bride.* Michigan: 1991.

Flusser, David. *Jewish Sources in Early Christianity.* New

York: Adama Press, 1987.

* Frankel, Ellen. *The Encyclopedia of Jewish Symbols*. London: Jason Aaronson, 1995.

— *The Five Books of Miriam*. San Francisco: Harper Collins, 1998.

Frazier, James. *The Golden Bough*. New York: Gramercy Books, 1981.

Freeman, James. *Manners and Customs of the Bible*. Plainfield, N.J.: Logos International, 1972 (Reprint).

Fruchtenbaum, Arnold. *Hebrew Christianity*. Washington D.C.: Canon Press, 1974.

— *Jesus Was a Jew*. Tustin, California: Ariel Press, 1981.

Gastor, Theodore. *Customs and Folkways of Jewish Life*. New York: W. Sloane Associates, 1955.

Geikie, Cunningham. *The Life and Words of Christ*. New York: D. Appleton and Company, 1886.

Gittelsohn, Roland. *The Extra Dimension - A Jewish View of Marriage*. New York: Union of American Hebrew Congregation, 1983.

Glasner, Mitch and Zhava. *The Fall Feasts of Israel*. Chicago, Illinois: Moody Press, 1987.

Glustrom, Simon. *The Language of Judaism*. London: Aronson, 1966.

Gold, Michael. *God, Love, Sex, and Family*. Northvale: Jason Aronson, 1998.

Goodenough, E. *Jewish Symbols in the Greco-Roman Period*. 1953. Ed. Jacob Neusner. New Jersey: Princeton University Press, 1988.

Goodspeed, E. *The Apocrypha, An American Translation*. New York: Vintage Books, Random House, 1938.

* Gower, Ralph. *The New Manners and Customs of Bible Times*. Chicago: Moody Press, 1987.

Graves, Robert and Raphael Patai. *Hebrew Myths - The Book of Genesis*. New York: Anchor Books Doubleday, 1963.

Greenberg, Rabbi Irving. *The Jewish Way*. New York: Simon and Schuster, 1988.

Greenwood, Glen and L. Scott. *A Marriage Made in Heaven.* Dallas: Word Publishing, 1990.

Grelot, Pierre. *Man and Wife in Scripture.* New York: Herder and Herder, 1964.

Grosvenor, M.B., Editor. *Everyday Life in Bible Times.* Pleasantville, N.Y.: Reader's Digest Association, 1997.

Habershon, Ada. *Types in the Old Testament.* 1916. Grand Rapids, Michigan: Kregel Publications, 1988.

Hareuveni, Nogah. *Nature in Our Biblical Heritage.* Translated from Hebrew by Helen Frenkley. Israel: Neot Kedumim Ltd., 1980.

— *Tree and Shrub in Our Biblical Heritage.* Translated from Hebrew by Helen Frenkley. Israel: Neot Kedumim Ltd., 1989.

Heaton, E.W. *Everyday Life in Old Testament Times.* New York: Chas. Scribner's Sons, 1956.

* Heschel, Abraham Joshua. *God in Search of Man.* New York: Farrer, Straus, and Giroux, 1955.

* — *The Prophets.* 2 vol. Grand Rapids: Harper Torchbooks, 1975.

* — *The Sabbath.* Canada: Harper Collins, 1951.

Holladay, W. *Long Ago God Spoke.* Minneapolis: Augsberg Fortress, 1995.

* Holtz, Barry. ed. *Back to the Sources, Reading the Classic Jewish Texts.* New York: Summit Books, 1984.

Huber, Robert, Editor. *The Bible Through the Ages.* Pleasantville, N.Y.: Reader's Digest Association, 1996.

Ilan, Tal. *Jewish Women in Greco-Roman Palestine.* Peabody, Mass.: Hendrickson Publishers, 1995.

Intrater, Asher. *Covenant Relationships.* Shippensburg: Destiny Image, 1989.

Intrater, Asher, and Dan Juster. *Israel, the Church, and the Last Days.* Shippensburg: Destiny Image, 1990.

Isaacs, R. and K. Olitzky. *Critical Documents of Jewish History.* London: Jason Aronson, 1995.

Jacob, Benno. *Genesis*. Edited and translated from German by Ernest and Walter Jacob. New York: KTAV, 1974

Jerimias, J. *Jerusalem in the Time of Jesus*. London: SCM, 1969.

Jones, Debbie, and Jackie Kendall. *Lady in Waiting*. Pennsylvania: Destiny Image, 1995.

Joseph, Arthur Samuel. *The Sound of the Soul*. Dearfield Beach, Florida: Health Communication Inc., 1996.

* Juengst, Sara. *Breaking Bread: The Spiritual Significance of Food*. Louisville: Westminster/John Knox Press, 1992.

Juster, Dan. *Jewish Roots*. Shippensburg, Pennsylvania: Destiny Image, 1995.

— *Jewishness and Jesus*. Madison: Inter Varsity Press, 1977.

Kaplan, A. *Waters of Eden*. New York: Union of Orthodox Jewish Congregations of America, 1982.

Keener, Craig. *The IVP Bible Background Commentary, New Testament*. Downer's Grove: Inter Varsity Press, 1993.

Keller, Werner. *The Bible as History*. New York: William Morrow and Co., 1981.

Kelley, Jack. *The Bride*. Salt Lake City, Utah: Meta Tauta Society.

Klinch, Arthur. *Home Life in Bible Times*. St. Louis: Concordia Publishing House, 1947.

Lacks, Roslyn. *Women and Judaism*. Garden City, New York: Doubleday and Company, 1980.

Lamsa, George. *Gospel Light*. San Francisco: Harper Collins, 1993.

— *Idioms in the Bible Explained*. San Francisco: Harper and Row, 1985.

— *My Neighbor Jesus*. San Antonio, Texas: Aramaic Bible Center, 1932.

— *New Testament Commentary*. Philadelphia: A.J. Holman Co., 1981.

— *Old Testament Light*. San Francisco: Harper Collins, 1936.

Lash, Jamie. *The Ancient Jewish Wedding*. Fort Lauderdale,

Florida: Love Song to the Messiah Assn., 1997.

Leibowitz, Nehama. *New Studies in Bereshit (Genesis).* Translated from Hebrew by Aryeh Newman. Jerusalem: Hemed Press, 1974.

— *New Studies in Shemot (Exodus) II.* Translated from Hebrew by Aryeh Newman. Jerusalem: Haomanim Press, 1976.

Levenson, Jon. *Sinai and Zion.* San Francisco: Harper and Row, 1985.

Levitt, Zola. *A Christian Love Story.* Dallas: Zola Levitt, 1978.

Lightfoot, John. *Hebraica.* 2 vol. "Commentary on the New Testament from the Talmud and Hebraica." Peabody: Hendrickson Publications, 1979.

Limburg, James. *Judaism, An Introduction for Christians.* Minneapolis: Augsburg Publishing, 1987.

Mackie, George M. *Bible Manners and Customs.* Old Tappan, New Jersey: Fleming H. Revell Company.

Matthews, Victor. *Manners and Customs in the Bible.* Peabody, Mass.: Hendrickson Publishers, 1988.

Maynard, Jill, Editor. *Illustrated Dictionary of Bible Life and Times.* Pleasantville, N.Y.: Reader's Digest Association, 1997.

Meier, Levi. *Ancient Secrets.* New York: Villard, 1996.

Meyers, Carol. "The Family in Early Israel." Browning 1-47.

Miller, Madeleine and Lane. *Harper's Encyclopedia of Bible Life.* Edison Castle Books, 1978.

Moldenke, Harold and Alma Moldenke. *Plants of the Bible.* New York: Dover Publications, 1952.

Mollenkott, V.R. *The Divine Feminine.* New York: The Crossland Publishing Company, 1983.

— *Women, Men, and the Bible.* Nashville: Abingdon Press, 1977.

Monson, James. *The Land Between.* Israel: Biblical Backgrounds, Inc., 1996.

Moore, George Foot. *Judaism in the First Centuries of the Christian Era: The Age of Tannaim.* 3 vols. 1927. Peabody Mass.: Hendrickson Publishers, 1997.

Mordechai, Avi Ben. *Signs in the Heavens*. Kila, MT: Millennium 7000 Communications International, 1999.

Morton, H.V. *In the Steps of the Master*. New York: Dodd, Mead, and Co., 1934.

Moseley, Ron. *Yeshua*. Maryland: Ebed Publications, 1996.

Murphey, Cecil. *The Dictionary of Biblical Literacy*. Nashville: Thomas Nelson Publishers, 1989.

Nadich, Judah. *Jewish Legends of the Second Commonwealth*. Philadelphia: The Jewish Publication Society of America, 1983.

National Geographic "In the Birthplace of Christianity", "Among the Shepherds of Bethlehem." vol. 50, December 1926.

National Geographic "Where Jesus Walked" by Howard LaFay. Volume 132, December 1967.

Neusner, Jacob. *A Midrash Reader*. Minneapolis: Fortress Press, 1990.

Nowell, Irene. *Women in the Old Testament*. Collegeville, Minnesota: The Liturgical Press, 1997.

Otwell, John H. *And Sarah Laughed*. Philadelphia: Westminster Press, 1977.

Packer, J. I, Merrill Tenney and W. White. *Nelson's Illustrated Encyclopedia of Bible Facts*. Nashville: Thomas Nelson Publishers, 1995.

Patai, Raphael. *Family, Love, and the Bible*. London: MacGibbon & Kee, 1960.

— *The Jewish Mind*. New York: Charles Scribner's Sons, 1977.

— *Man and Temple*. London: Thomas Nelson and Sons, 1947.

— *The Messiah Texts*. Detroit: Wayne State University Press, 1979.

— *On Jewish Folklore*. Detroit: Wayne State University Press, 1983.

— *Sex and Family in the Bible and the Middle East*. Garden City, New York: Doubleday and Company, 1959.

Patterson, Dorothy. "A Treasure to Protect." pg. 716. Women's Devotional Bible. NIV. Zondervan, 1990.

Patton, William. *Bible Wines, or Laws of Fermentation and Wines of the Ancients.* USA: Sane Press.

Perdue, Leo G. "The Household, Old Testament Theology, and Contemporary Hemeneutics." Browning 223-257.

— "The Israelite and Early Jewish Family: Summary and Conclusions." Browning 163-222.

Perry, Joy. "Garden of Eden Analysis." Personal Correspondence, 1996.

Peterson, Galen. *The Everlasting Tradition.* Grand Rapids, MI: Kregel Publications, 1995.

Pfeiffer, Charles, et. al. *The New Combined Bible Dictionary and Concordance.* Grand Rapids: Baker Book, 1961.

Plaut, W.G. ed. *The Torah - A Modern Commentary.* New York: Jewish Publication Society, 1981.

Pryor, Dwight. *Our Hebrew Lord: Discovering the Historical Jesus.* Dayton, Ohio: Center For Judaic-Christian Studies, 1993.

Radin, Max. *Jews Among the Greeks and Romans.* Philadelphia, 1915.

— *The Life of the People In Biblical Times.* Philadelphia: The Jewish Publication Society of America, 1948.

Ragen, Naomi. *Sotah.* New York: Crown Publishers, 1992.

Ratcliff, J.D. *Your Body and How It Works.* Delacorte Press, 1975.

Richman, Chiam. *A House of Prayer for All Nations.* Jerusalem: The Temple Institute and Carta, 1997.

Rihbany, Abraham. *The Syrian Christ.* New York: Houghton Mifflin, 1910.

Rogers, Aaron. *The Messianic Jewish Book of Why?* 2 vols. Sandy, Utah: Camden Court Publishers, 1996.

Sabourin, Leopold. *The Names and Titles of Jesus - Themes of Biblical Theology.* New York: The MacMillan Company, 1967.

Sacks, Stuart. *Hebrews Through a Hebrew's Eyes.* Baltimore, Maryland: Lederer Messianic Publishers, 1995.

Sanders, E.P. *Jesus and Judaism.* London: SCM, 1985

Schechter, S. *Aspects of Rabbinic Theology*. New York: Schocken, 1961.

Scherer, George. *The Eastern Colour of the Bible*. London: The National S.S. Union, 1932.

Schneerson, M.M. *From Exile to Redemption*. vol I. Brooklyn, New York: Kehot Publication Society, 1992.

— *Toward a Meaningful Life*. New York: William Morrow and Company, 1995.

Schürer, E. *The History of the Jewish People in the Time of Jesus Christ*. 1891. 6 vols. Reprint. Peabody, Mass.: Hendrickson, 1993.

Simpson, A.B. *Divine Emblems*. Pennsylvania: Christian Publications, 1995.

Slemming, C.W. *These are the Garments*. Fort Washington, Pennsylvania: Christian Literature Crusade, 1995.

Smith, William. *A Dictionary of the Bible*. Nashville: Thomas Nelson Publishers, 1986.

Starbird, Margaret: *The Woman With the Alabaster Jar*. Santa Fe, New Mexico: Bear and Company, Inc., 1993.

* Stern, David. *Jewish New Testament Commentary*. Clarksville: Jewish New Testament Publications, 1992.

Stone, Samuel J. "The Church's One Foundation" 1866. Used by permission of Oxford University Press. From "Varied Harmonizations."

Strong, James. *Strong's Exhaustive Concordance of the Bible*. Peabody, Mass.: Hendrickson Publishers.

Telushkin, Joseph. *Jewish Literacy*. New York: William Morrow and Company, 1991.

Terrien, Samuel. *Till the Heart Sings - A Biblical Theology of Manhood and Womanhood*. Philadelphia: Fortress Press, 1985.

The Jewish Catalog. Richard Siegal, Michael and Sharon Strassfield, editors.

The Sabbath. Samuel Dresner. Philadelphia: Jewish Pub. Society of America, 1973.

Thompson, J.A. *Handbook of Life in Bible Times*. Madison, Wisconsin: Inter Varsity, 1986.

Thomson, Wm. *The Land and the Book.* 3 vols. New York: Harper and Brothers, 1880.

Trepp, Leo. *The Complete Book of Jewish Observance.* New York: Behrman House/Summit Books, 1980.

Tubb, Jonathan. *Bible Lands.* New York: Alfred Knoff, 1991.

Vander Laan, Ray. *Echoes of His Presence.* Colorado Springs, Colorado: Focus on the Family Publishing, 1996.

Vermes, G. *Jesus and the World of Judaism.* London: SCM, 1983.

Vine, W.E. *Vine's Complete Expository Dictionary of Old and New Testament Words.* Nashville: Thomas Nelson Publishers, 1984.

Walker, Winifred. *All the Plants of the Bible.* New York: Harper and Brothers Publishers, 1943.

Ward, B. *Healing Foods From the Bible.* Baca Raton: Globe, 1994.

White, Ellen. *Christ's Object Lessons.* New York: Pacific Press, 1900.

Wiersbe, Warren W. *Be Committed.* Wheaton, Illinois: Victor Books, 1993.

Wight, Fred. *Manners and Customs of Bible Lands.* Chicago: Moody Press, 1953.

Willmington, H.L. *Book of Bible Lists.* Wheaton, Illinois: Tyndale House Publishers, 1987.

* Wilson, Marvin. *Our Father Abraham.* Grand Rapids: Eerdmans Publishing Co., 1989.

Wilson, W. *Wilson's Old Testament Word Studies.* Peabody, Mass.: Henrickson Publishers.

Wolpe, David. *In Speech and in Silence: The Jewish Quest for God.* New York: Henry Holt, 1992.

Wright, G.E. ed. *Great People of the Bible and How They Lived.* Pleasantville, N.Y.: Reader's Digest Association, 1974.

Yonge, C.D. Translator. *The Works of Philo.* Peabody, Mass.: Henrickson Publishers, 1997.

Young, Brad H. *Jesus and His Jewish Parables.* Mahwah:

Paulist, 1989.

—— *Jesus the Jewish Theologian.* Massachusetts: Hendrickson, 1995.

— *The Jewish Background of the Lord's Prayer.* Austin: Center for Judaic Christian Studies, 1984.

Young, Woody, and Chuck Missler. *Countdown to Eternity.* San Juan Capistrano: Joy Publishing, 1992.

Zborowski, M. and Herzog, E. *Life is With People: The Culture of the Shetl.* New York: Schocken, 1962.

*Starred books are highly recommended.